THE AMAZING
ANIMAL
—KINGDOM—

Brown Watson

ENGLAND

CONTENTS

CONTENTS

CONTENTS

DINOSAURS

and other Prehistoric Animals

by Colin Clark

Illustrated by Geoff Campion

FROM WATER TO DRY LAND

Life on Earth began in the seas around 3,500 million years ago. Not until 420 million years ago did plants, insects and worms move onto dry land. The first fish appeared 400 million years ago, and 20 million years later some fish had developed the ability to move about on land. They were the amphibians, the first animals with backbones to walk on land.

ERYOPS (EER-ee-ops)
300 million years ago

This 1.5-metre-long amphibian could live in desert conditions, its thick, tough skin helping it retain moisture. It was probably slow-moving and clumsy on land. In water, it could catch smaller amphibians and reptiles. It also laid its eggs in water.

DIADECTES (die-a-DEK-tees)
260 million years ago

This heavily-built creature was fully adapted to life on land. Indeed, some scientists argue that it was not an amphibian at all, but one of the first reptiles. It was 3 metres long, and its blunt, peg-like teeth tell us that it was a plant-eater.

EOGYRINUS (EE-o-jie-RINE-us)
300 million years ago

Eogyrinus was a 4-metre-long amphibian, with a broad, flat head and many small teeth. Its legs were too short to keep its body off the ground and it would have moved about very slowly on land. Its strong tail enabled it to swim well.

THE FIRST LAND MONSTERS

Some strange-looking creatures roamed on Earth in the 70 million year period when amphibians were the dominant species. Shown here are two amphibians, and the Edaphosaurus, an early reptile. Around 285 million years ago, reptiles took over as the dominant form of life.

DIPLOCAULUS (dip-lo-CAWL-us)
280-230 million years ago

Living mainly at the bottom of pools and only occasionally coming onto the land, the Diplocaulus was about 60 cm long. We do not know why it had such a strange, wedge-shaped head.

MASTODONSAURUS
(MAST-o-don-SAWR-us)
270 million years ago

This beast resembled a huge frog, with a head which was over a metre long, bigger than the head of any other amphibian (a creature which lives on land but lays its eggs in water), living or extinct. Its small, weak legs made it awkward on land.

EDAPHOSAURUS

(e-DAF-o-SAWR-us)

270 million years ago

These odd animals had a powerful skull, and, making use of their crushing teeth, they probably fed on shellfish from swampy areas. Their 'sail' helped both to heat and cool their 3½ metre-long body.

STRANGE CREATURES FROM THE SEA

The Earth's first creatures lived in water. Some of them are shown here. The largest animal alive today also lives in the sea. It is the Blue Whale, which is actually the largest creature that has ever lived. It can grow to over 33 metres in length, and weigh around 190,000 kilos.

NOTHOSAURUS (NOT-o-SAWR-us)
200 million years ago

This long-necked, long-tailed reptile was a great fish-eater. It grew up to 6 metres in length, had webbed feet, and could move about on land.

DINICHTHYS (die-NICK-this)
200 million years ago

The name of this armour-plated hunter means 'terrible fish'! It grew to a length of 10 metres, and it had an enormous mouth, full of vicious teeth.

PLESIOSAUR (PLEEZ-i-o-SAWR)
150 million years ago

This beast was a descendant of the Nothosaurus. The name means 'swan-lizard', but really they looked more like long-necked turtles. While swimming, they kept their head up out of the water.

BASILOSAURUS (BA-sil-o-SAWR-us)
35 million years ago

An early form of whale, 28 metres long, the Basilosaurus looked like a giant sea snake with a mouth containing 44 very sharp teeth.

FIERCE HUNTERS

The story of prehistory is filled with the names of the most terrifying carnivorous (meat-eating) animals. Four fierce carnivores are pictured below: a reptile; a bird; and two mammals.

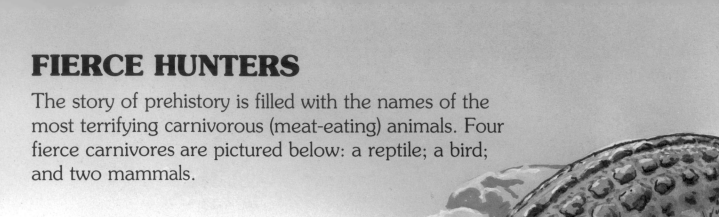

ORNITHOSUCHUS
(OR-nith-o-sook-us)
240 million years ago

This is one of the very first two-legged, flesh-eating dinosaurs. 3 or 4 metres long and 1 metre high, Ornithosuchus was a highly efficient killer of the slow-moving plant-eaters of the period. This ferocious reptile was armoured with bony plates just under its skin.

PHORUSRHACOS
(FOR-us-RA-kos)
40 million years ago

For a period of about 20 million years, in both what is now Europe and South America, the largest meat-eating species were giant, flightless birds. The one shown here was 1.5 metres tall, and was fast enough to run down the plant-eating mammals on which it fed.

12

ANDREWSARCHUS
(AN-drew-SARK us)
50 million years ago

This 'bear-dog' was like a giant, horse-sized wolf. It was 4 metres long, and its skull alone was about a metre in length, five times the size of the largest tiger's today. It used its broad, bone-crunching cheek teeth to tear the flesh from carcasses.

PAKICETUS (PACK-i-SEET-us)
50 million years ago

Like the Basilosaurus on page 11, the much older Pakicetus was also an early type of whale. It was around 1.8 metres long, and had arms and legs that were like the 'paddles' found on today's seals. Originating from dog-like land-dwelling creatures, this marine mammal was a fearsome hunter.

THE 'UNREAL' LIZARDS

When the bones of some of these great dinosaurs were first discovered, people could not believe that such vast creatures ever really lived on Earth. The name Apatosaurus, meaning 'Unreal Lizard', was given to one particular giant.

APATOSAURUS (a-PAT-o-SAWR-us)
150 million years ago

Another name for this plant-eater is Brontosaurus, or 'Thunder Lizard'. 21 metres long, weighing over 30,000 kilos, it must have made a noise like thunder when it moved!

ALLOSAURUS (AL-lo-SAWR-us)
150 million years ago

Although it was less than half the size of a Brontosaurus, this fierce, flesh-eating dinosaur, over 9 metres long, could easily kill the larger, slow-moving, defenceless beasts.

T E LONGEST AND T E LARGEST

Some of the plant-eating dinosaurs grew to a truly enormous size. Much of their lives was spent in lakes, where the water helped to support their weight.

DIPLODOCUS (dip-lo-DOK-us)
150 million years ago

The longest dinosaur measured nearly 30 metres from its head to the tip of its long tail. Like the other giant plant-eaters, it stayed in water for most of the time, out of reach of its fierce enemies.

BRACHIOSAURUS
(BRAK-i-o-SAWR-us)
100 million years ago

This was the largest of all dinosaurs, with front legs that were longer than its back legs. Nearly 25 metres long, weighing 50,000 kilos, with its neck lifted up it would have been able to look straight into the third-storey window of a house!

ARMOURED DINOSAURS

Some of the slower-moving species of dinosaur were only able to survive by developing various kinds of armour. Some of them became like living tanks!

STEGOSAURUS (steg-o-SAWR-us)
140 million years ago

Up to 10 metres long, and sometimes weighing 10,000 kilos, this giant plant-eater had two rows of sharp, bony plates on its back, and a tail armed with four strong spikes.

SCELIDOSAURUS
(SEL-id-o-SAWR-us)
170 million years ago

One of the first of the armoured dinosaurs, the Scelidosaurus was about 3½ metres long, with bony plates all down its back.

THE FIRST FLYING REPTILES

While the giant reptiles ruled the dry land, other species took to the air. They were called Pterosaurs, which means 'wing reptiles'. Their wings were made of sheets of skin, fastened to an extra-long finger on each 'hand', just like the wings on bats today.

DIMORPHODON (die-MORF-o-don)
160 million years ago

This was one of the earliest of the flying reptiles, and its head was very large in comparison to its body. These creatures probably hung upside down from rocky ledges, or tree branches, when they were at rest.

RHAMPHORHYNCHUS
(RAM-fo-RINK-us)
160 million years ago

Little bigger than a crow, this pterosaur had a long, thin tail which ended in a leaf-shaped fin. This helped it to control its movements in the air. It used its forward-pointing teeth to spear its prey.

PTERODACTYLUS (ter-o-DAKT-il-us)
140 million years ago

Sometimes no bigger than a sparrow, the pterodactyl had hardly any tail, but its wings were much longer in proportion to its body. Pterodactyls lived in flocks, and their skin was closely wrinkled, and perhaps brightly coloured.

BIG CLAWS

The dinosaurs pictured below all made particular use of their claws, which were often huge. They were also ruthless hunters, and, contrary to the popular view of dinosaurs as slow-moving beasts, two of these species were very fast indeed on their feet.

BARYONYX (ba-REE-on-ix)
124 million years ago

The name means 'heavy claw', and this dinosaur was about 10 metres long. When it stood on its hind legs, it would have been able to reach up about 4 metres. Baryonyx had a head like a crocodile's. It ate fish, and also other dinosaurs, ripping them open with its largest claw.

DEINONYCHUS (die-no-NEEK-us)
110 million years ago

About 1.5 metres high, and 3 metres long, these intelligent dinosaurs specialised in hunting in packs. They ran very fast on their two hind legs, using their stiff tail to balance them. They killed their prey by slashing them with the enlarged, scythe-like claws on the back feet.

VELOCIRAPTOR
(VEE-loss-ee-RAP-tore)
80 million years ago

The name means 'speedy robber'. It had well-developed sickle claws, and moved fast, hunting in packs. The fossilised remains have been found of a Velociraptor locked in its death struggle with a Protoceratops, one of the 'Horned Faces' mentioned on pages 34-35.

THE 'BIRD-FEET' AND THE 'DUCK-BILLS'

Two amazing groups of dinosaurs are the 'ornithopods', meaning the dinosaurs with 'bird feet', like the Iguanodon pictured below, and the 'hadrosaurs', which were dinosaurs with beaks like a duck's bill, such as Corythosaurus.

IGUANODON (ig-yew-AHN-o-don)
100 million years ago

5½ metres high and 11 metres long, the Iguanodon moved swiftly over the ground on its back legs, with their great three-clawed feet. When attacked, it used its long thumbs like daggers.

CORYTHOSAURUS

(ko-RITH-o-SAWR-us)

100 million years ago

These 'duck-bills' had webbed feet and mouths containing about 1,000 teeth! The one shown here was gigantic, over 12 metres long, with a bony crest like a helmet on its head.

THE ORIGINAL SEA SERPENT

Long, long ago, the seas were home for two different types of giant dinosaur. One type, like the Elasmosaurus shown here, had a neck twice as long as its body, and was probably the very first sea serpent. The other type, like the Kronosaurus, had a large, strong head.

ELASMOSAURUS (ee-LAZ-mo-SAWR-us)
100 million years ago

Because of its neck, the Elasmosaurus grew to a total length of 14½ metres. Its paddles, though, were short, so it was not a fast swimmer. It caught fish by swinging its head about swiftly.

KRONOSAURUS (KRO-no-SAWR-us)
100 million years ago

The head of this frightening beast was over 3 metres long, and it had the biggest mouth of any dinosaur. A man could have passed through it very easily. In appearance, it was like a 13-metre-long crocodile!

THE 'HORRIBLE LIZARDS'

Around 80 million years ago, there arose a species of
dinosaur called 'deinodonts', which means 'terrible teeth'.
They were blood-thirsty predators, who fed on the herds
of plant-eating reptiles which lived in the ferny forests
and swamps of the time.

GORGOSAURUS (gor-go-SAWR-us)
100 million years ago

Over 3½ metres long, this flesh-
eating reptile was a savage beast.
Its name means 'horrible lizard',
and it was probably very clumsy in
its movements. Most likely, its
main food consisted of the
carcasses of already dead
dinosaurs.

TYRANNOSAURUS
(tie-RAN-o-SAWR-us)
80 million years ago

Its name means 'tyrant reptile'. 6 metres in height and over 15 metres long, it was the largest flesh-eating animal that has ever lived on land. Its front legs were so short they could not even reach its mouth, and it carried its long tail upright as it moved, in order to balance the weight of its enormous body.

THE 'CROOKED LIZARDS'

A new species of dinosaur was descended from the Stegosaurus pictured on pages 18. The name given to this species was 'ankylosaur', meaning 'crooked lizard', because of the curved ribs of all these strange creatures.

SCOLOSAURUS (SCOL-o-SAWR-us)
100 million years ago

About 6 metres long, with an armour-plated back, its short legs kept this dinosaur close to the ground. It was only in danger when enemies, like the Gorgosaurus, shown on pages 28-29, were able to turn it over, exposing its unprotected stomach.

ANKYLOSAURUS (an-KILE-o-SAWR-us)
80 million years ago

This was a massive, slow-moving beast, over 7 metres long. Its back was covered with bony plates, which had long spines at the edges. Its head was also armoured, and its tail ended in a heavy, bony club, which could break the leg of a Tyrannosaurus.

FLYING LIZARD TO FIRST BIRD

100 million years passed from the time of the winged reptiles shown on pages 20-21 to the last appearance in the skies above the Earth of the 'flying dragon' called the Pteranodon, which had a wing-span of over 8 metres.

ARCHAEOPTERYX (ARK-ee-OP-ter-ix)
140 million years ago

This was an extraordinary creature, halfway between a reptile and a bird. It had the teeth of a reptile, the long tail of a lizard, proper hands on the front of its wings, and it was covered in coloured feathers.

PTERANODON (ter-AN-o-don)
60 million years ago

The strange head of this creature
extended to the rear in a bony
comb. Its long, pointed snout was
toothless. It flew by gliding, rather
than by flapping its wings, so it must
have swooped low over the sea in
order to spear the fish that it ate.

THE 'HORNED FACES'

About 80 million years ago, herds of great four-footed dinosaurs roamed slowly over the plains. They had wide, bony collars round their monstrous heads, which were armed with long horns. They were the 'Ceratops', or 'Horned Faces'.

TRICERATOPS (try-SER-a-tops)
80 million years ago

As the name suggests, this great beast had three horns, two long ones above the eyes, and one on the nose. It was 8 metres long, weighed over 9,000 kilos, and had a huge, hooked beak.

MONOCLONIUS (mon-o-KLONE-ee-us)
100 million years ago

One of the earliest horned
dinosaurs, Monoclonius grew to a
length of over 5 metres. Its head
measured 2 metres from the point
of its horn to the back of its bony,
frilled, neck collar.

STYRACOSAURUS
(sty-RAK-o-SAWR-us)
80 million years ago

As well as a half-metre-long horn on
its nose, the Styracosaurus also had
long, sharp horns round its neck frill.
Like the other 'horned faces' though,
it was a placid plant-eater.

'HELMET HEADS'

Other dinosaurs in the group known as 'hadrosaurs' included some with heads which were even more strangely shaped than the head of the Corythosaurus on page 25. Indeed, another name for this whole group is the 'Helmet Heads'.

PARASAUROLOPHUS

(PAR-a-sawr-o-LOWF-us)
80 million years ago

This 10-metre-long hadrosaur had one of the most unusual 'helmets'. Its crest was full of air passages which were linked to the nose and mouth. When Parasaurolophus breathed out strongly, the air which was forced through these passages made a loud, bellowing sound.

TSINTAOSAURUS

(SIN-ta-o-SAWR-us)
80 million years ago

This one's crest featured a single, forward-facing bone. Hadrosaurs moved in herds, laid their eggs in communal nesting sites, and looked after their young in nurseries, until they could fend for themselves.

LAMBEOSAURUS

(LAM-bee-o-SAWR-us)
80 million years ago

Part of the 'helmet' of this strange-looking creature consisted of a 'plate' set on its side. Hadrosaurs walked on two feet, and had short, strong arms. Their duck-billed mouths had as many as 2,000 teeth, but they ate only plant food.

GIANT PLANT-EATERS

50 million years after the hadrosaurs pictured on the previous pages, a number of great plant-eating mammals roamed the Earth. They were strange-looking beasts, and the three shown here each had some partial resemblance to animals we know today.

ARSINOTHERIUM
(AR-sin-o-THEER-ee-um)
35 million years ago

This looked rather like a rhinoceros, except for the fact that it had two enormous horns side by side on its snout. Their mouths had 44 teeth, with which they crushed the juicy swamp plants on which they fed.

CHALICOTHERIUM
(CHAL-i-ko-THEER-ee-um)
50 to 1 million years ago

One of the strangest-looking plant-eaters ever, it had a horse-like head, long arms, large claws, and it was a man's height, though 3 metres long. The Chalicotherium walked on its knuckles, like gorillas today, and it survived for 50 million years, finally dying out in Africa in the time of early Man.

BALUCHITHERIUM
(ba-LOO-ki-THEER-ee-um)
30 million years ago

This hornless giant lived in herds, and was the biggest mammal ever to have walked on Earth. 5 metres high at the shoulder and 8 metres long, it weighed as much as 8 rhinos. Its vast head, with two huge teeth projecting down from its upper jaw, was set on a long neck, and it could feed off treetops almost 8 metres high.

'DAWN HORSE' TO 'THUNDER BEAST'

About 60 million years ago, the dinosaurs disappeared. We still do not really understand why this happened so suddenly. After ruling the Earth for 200 million years, their place was taken by mammals, like those pictured on the previous pages and below. Mammals are warm-blooded creatures which give birth to living young. Man is a mammal.

EOHIPPUS (ee-o-HIPP-us)
36 million years ago

The first horse is called Eohippus, which means 'Dawn Horse'. It was about the size of a fox, its neck was short, and it stood on tiny hoofs. It was well fitted for survival, as it could run fast, and hide easily in the shadows.

BRONTOTHERIUM
(bron-toe-THEER-ee-um)
25 million years ago

An early relative of today's rhinoceros, the Brontotherium, or 'Thunder Beast', was a clumsy, plant-eating animal, over 4 metres long, with hoofs and horns, and a brain no bigger than an orange.

MEGATHERIUM
(MEG-a-THEER-ee-um)
2 million years ago

Its name means 'Great Beast', and it grew to a length of over 7 metres. Though it was bigger than the largest elephant, the Megatherium could stand on its hind legs in order to eat the leaves in the tree-tops.

GIANT MAMMALS, GIANT BIRD

Some early relatives of animals we know today were gigantic. Shown below are three mammal giants, and one truly remarkable bird.

ALTICAMELUS (AL-tee-ca-MEL-us)
20 million years ago

The camel that crosses our deserts once had a relative that looked like a giraffe! Alticamelus (the name means 'high camel') was 4 metres high, with a long neck for feeding on treetops.

DIATRYMA (DIE-a-TRI-ma)
50 million years ago

In Brazil today, there is a bird called the cariama. It is a type of crane. The Diatryma was an early relative. Though unable to fly, it was a strong runner, with an eagle's beak. It was 2 metres high!

INDRICOTHERIUM
(in-DRIK-o-THEER-ee-um)
30 million years ago

Also an early rhinoceros, but even bigger than the Brontotherium on pages 40, this was 5 metres high, one of the largest land animals ever. It had no horns, and lived in small herds, eating leaves.

DINOHYUS (DINE-o-HIE-us)
20 million years ago

Believe it or not, even though the Dinohyus was as big as a large bull, it was a pig! It was nearly 2 metres high, and its back was covered with a bristly mane.

SABRE-TOOTHED KILLERS

During the long period from around 20 to 5 million years ago, grasslands spread over much of the Earth. Giant plant-eaters, like Chalicotherium shown on page 38, flourished. So did horses and antelopes. In pursuit of them came big hunting cats, with their long sabre-teeth.

NIMRAVIDES
(nim-RAH-vi-DEEZ)
10 million years ago

This early sabre-toothed cat attacked large slow-moving creatures such as mammoths. Its teeth could cut easily through the tough skin of a plant-eater, even though the victim might be much bigger than the hunter.

THYLACOSMILUS
(THIGH-la-ko-SMY-lus)
10 million years ago

This South American sabre-tooth was not really a cat at all, just a very good copy of one! A meat-eater, with the same stabbing teeth, it was a marsupial; meaning that its young were born live, but so tiny that they had to be carried in their mother's pouch until they were developed enough to survive on their own.

SMILODON (SMY-lo-don)
2 million years ago

The enormous, 15-centimetre-long fangs of this heavy beast could pierce the thickest skin. Smilodon's lower jaw could drop open into a right angle in order to clear the great upper teeth. They probably killed their prey by biting a chunk out of them and then waiting for them to bleed to death.

45

EARLY ELEPHANTS

Elephants appeared about 50 million years ago. They were little bigger than pigs at first, with short tusks and no trunk. About 20 million years later, elephants split into two different groups. Platybelodon was a member of one group. In the other group, there was Deinotherium, and, later, until about 10,000 years ago, the Mammoth. Today's Indian and African elephants are their descendants, but, tragically, very few are left alive.

DEINOTHERIUM
(DIE-no-THEER-ee-um)
15 million years ago

About 5 metres high at the shoulder, and much taller than today's elephants, Deinotherium had a long, flexible trunk. Its tusks were on its lower jaw, curving backwards under its chin. It probably used them for scraping the bark off trees.

PLATYBELODON
(plat-ee-BELL-o-don)
5 million years ago

This beast had not only two short, sharp tusks, one on each side of its trunk, but also two broad, flat, shovel-like tusks in its lower jaw. It was about 2 metres tall, and lived on the plants that it 'shovelled' out of the muddy ground.

WOOLLY MAMMOTH

(MAM-mohth)

5 million to 100,000 years ago

The North American Mammoth was the largest elephant ever. It was about 4 metres high at the shoulders, with gigantic curving tusks. Mammoths were covered in long hair and fur, and had a layer of fat beneath the skin to keep them warm in cold conditions. The Woolly Mammoth, which was hunted for food by cave men, survived longest in Siberia.

'LEFT-OVERS' FROM THE PAST

Some animals today look much the same as they did in prehistoric times. They have survived for millions and millions of years with very little change.

COELACANTH

This fish dates back to 300 million years ago. Until just over 50 years ago, it was thought to be extinct – like the dinosaurs. Then, one was found off the coast of South Africa, and others have been seen since.

TUATARA

These lizard-like reptiles can be found in New Zealand, and are the only ones left of a group that lived 170 million years ago. The name means 'having spines', as the tuatara has a row of spiny scales all down its back.

TURTLES and TORTOISES

They are the oldest type of living reptiles, and have been on earth for around 175 million years! The proper name for all of them is turtle, but the types that live on land are usually called tortoises.

CROCODILES

Crocodiles and alligators are a group that roamed the world 100 million years ago. They haven't changed much. If you want to know which is which, look at their closed mouths. You can see a crocodile's long teeth, but not an alligator's.

49

SHARKS
and
WHALES
and other Strange Creatures of the Sea

by Rupert Matthews and Colin Clark
Illustrated by Jim Channell

THE GIANT SHARKS

All sharks' fins are quite rigid, and act as stabilisers, keeping them steady in the water. These, the largest sharks of all, are actually no danger to swimmers, nor even to other fish! They feed on tiny sea animals and plants, called plankton, which drift around in the world's oceans. All three species shown here are very rare. Scientists still do not know for certain how long they live, nor how large they grow.

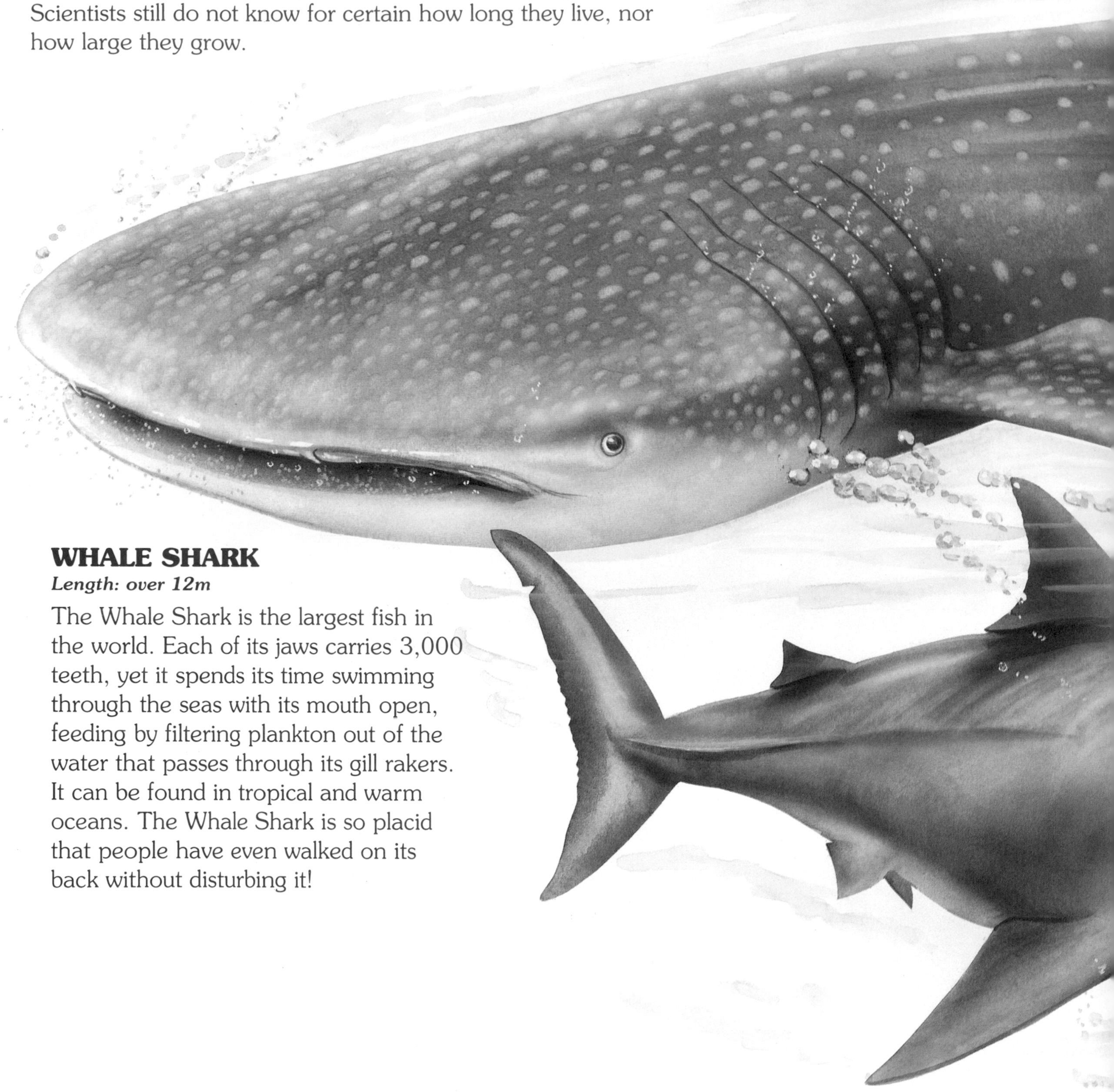

WHALE SHARK

Length: over 12m

The Whale Shark is the largest fish in the world. Each of its jaws carries 3,000 teeth, yet it spends its time swimming through the seas with its mouth open, feeding by filtering plankton out of the water that passes through its gill rakers. It can be found in tropical and warm oceans. The Whale Shark is so placid that people have even walked on its back without disturbing it!

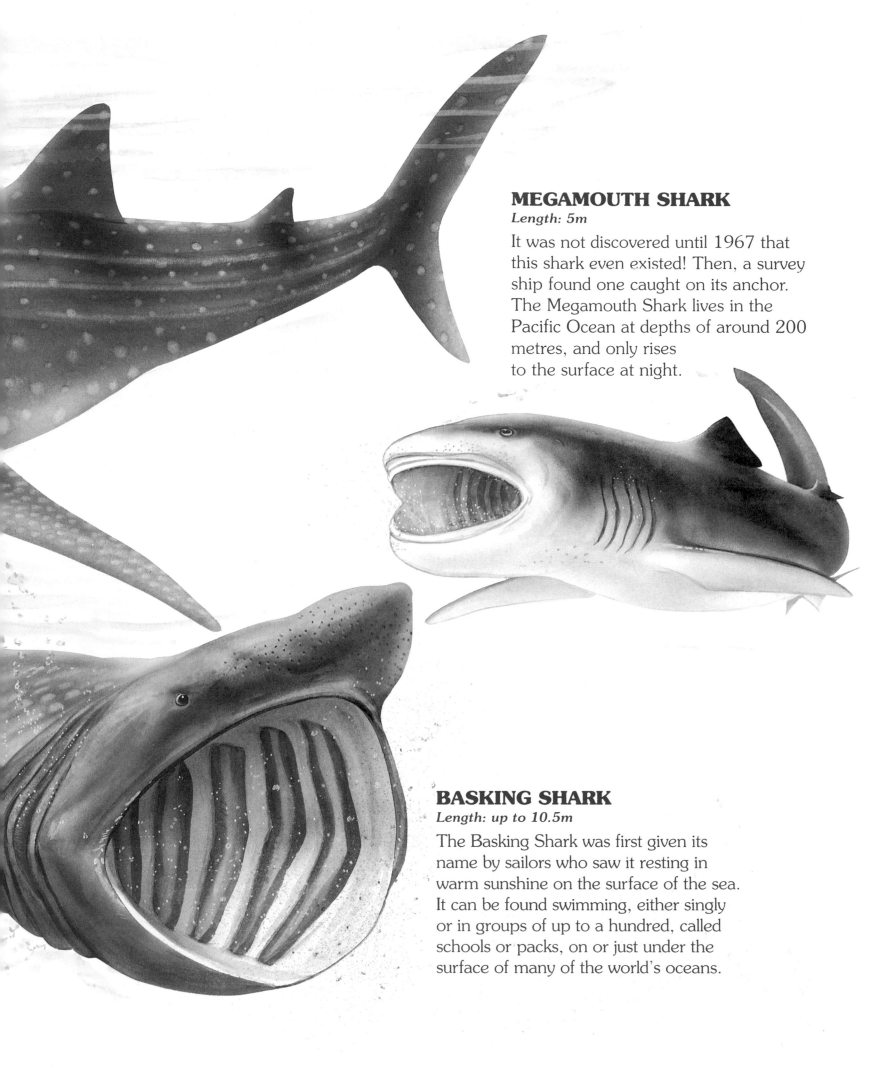

MEGAMOUTH SHARK
Length: 5m

It was not discovered until 1967 that this shark even existed! Then, a survey ship found one caught on its anchor. The Megamouth Shark lives in the Pacific Ocean at depths of around 200 metres, and only rises to the surface at night.

BASKING SHARK
Length: up to 10.5m

The Basking Shark was first given its name by sailors who saw it resting in warm sunshine on the surface of the sea. It can be found swimming, either singly or in groups of up to a hundred, called schools or packs, on or just under the surface of many of the world's oceans.

53

TERROR AT SEA

The larger sharks, because they feed on seals and other sea creatures, usually swim near the surface of the water where their prey is to be found. Their tails tend to be big in comparison to their powerful bodies. They travel thousands of kilometres in search of food, which they can detect by smell from far, far away. Only when they are close, do their eyes guide them in their onslaught. These sharks will attack human beings.

MACKEREL or PORBEAGLE SHARK
Length: about 3m

The name 'porbeagle' comes from the Cornish dialect and is of unknown origin. This ferocious predator can be found in open waters in the Atlantic and south Pacific Oceans, and in the Mediterranean and Barents Seas. A large, powerful fish, the Mackerel Shark, as its name would suggest, feeds in large numbers on mackerel, and on squid.

54

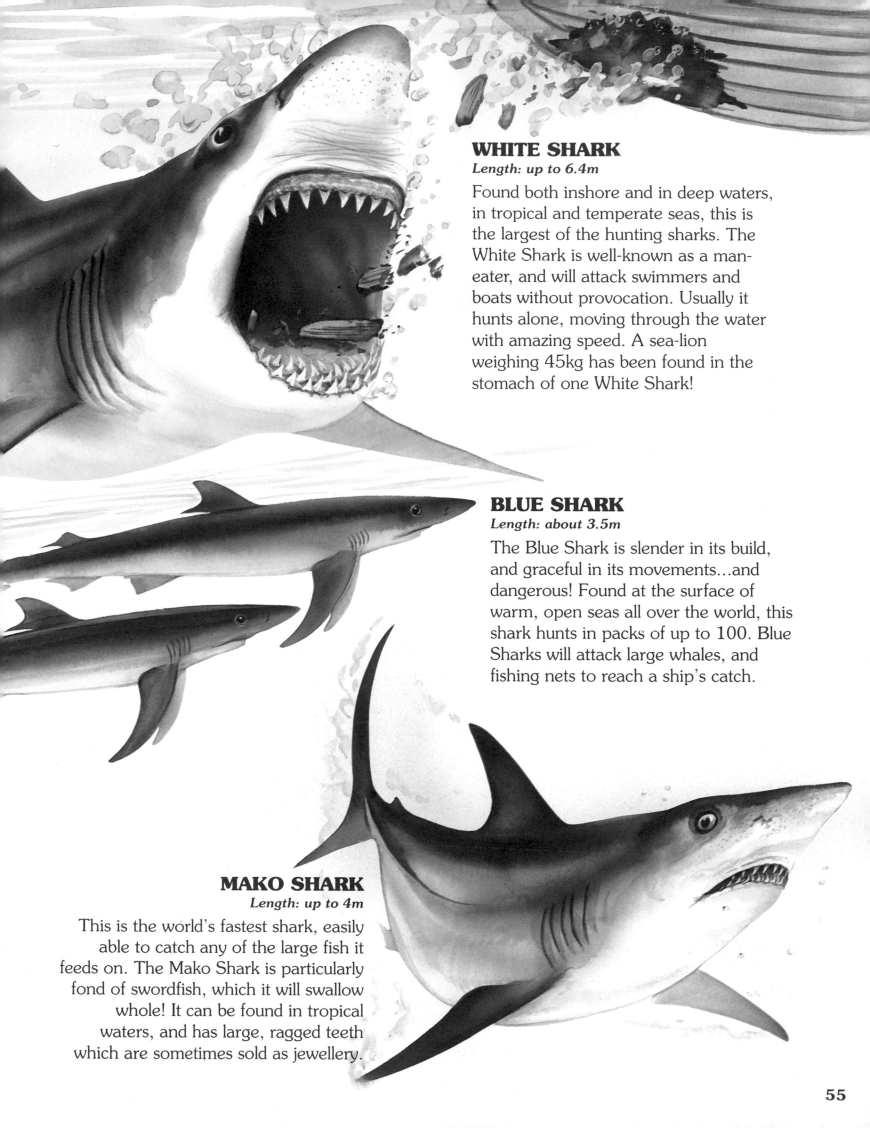

WHITE SHARK
Length: up to 6.4m

Found both inshore and in deep waters, in tropical and temperate seas, this is the largest of the hunting sharks. The White Shark is well-known as a man-eater, and will attack swimmers and boats without provocation. Usually it hunts alone, moving through the water with amazing speed. A sea-lion weighing 45kg has been found in the stomach of one White Shark!

BLUE SHARK
Length: about 3.5m

The Blue Shark is slender in its build, and graceful in its movements...and dangerous! Found at the surface of warm, open seas all over the world, this shark hunts in packs of up to 100. Blue Sharks will attack large whales, and fishing nets to reach a ship's catch.

MAKO SHARK
Length: up to 4m

This is the world's fastest shark, easily able to catch any of the large fish it feeds on. The Mako Shark is particularly fond of swordfish, which it will swallow whole! It can be found in tropical waters, and has large, ragged teeth which are sometimes sold as jewellery.

COASTAL KILLERS

Coastal sharks spend most of their time swimming slowly in waters close to shore. When attacking prey, they move quickly, but they give up easily if the chase is long. All three sharks shown here can be dangerous to man, as they will often come close to bathing beaches.

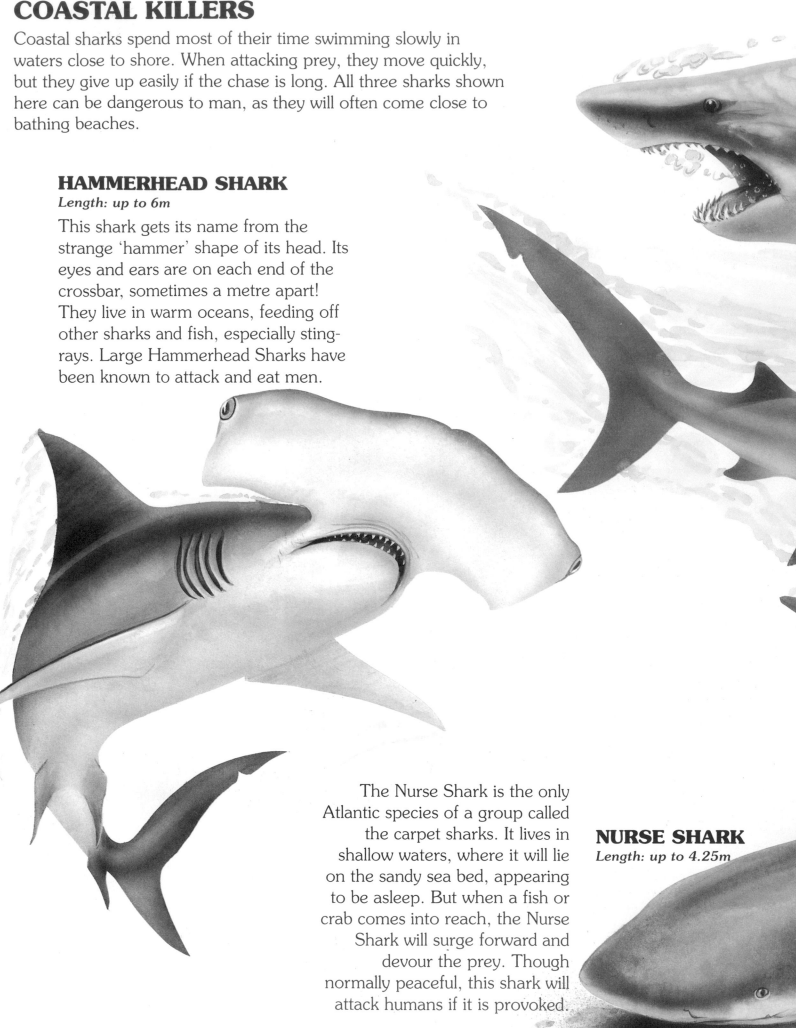

HAMMERHEAD SHARK

Length: up to 6m

This shark gets its name from the strange 'hammer' shape of its head. Its eyes and ears are on each end of the crossbar, sometimes a metre apart! They live in warm oceans, feeding off other sharks and fish, especially stingrays. Large Hammerhead Sharks have been known to attack and eat men.

The Nurse Shark is the only Atlantic species of a group called the carpet sharks. It lives in shallow waters, where it will lie on the sandy sea bed, appearing to be asleep. But when a fish or crab comes into reach, the Nurse Shark will surge forward and devour the prey. Though normally peaceful, this shark will attack humans if it is provoked.

NURSE SHARK

Length: up to 4.25m

TIGER SHARK

Length: up to 6m

The huge Tiger Shark gets its name from the stripes on its back when it is young. It is found throughout tropical seas, and, next to the great White Shark, it is probably the most aggressive and dangerous of all. Tiger Sharks are especially known for their numbers and ferocity off the coasts of Australia.

BULL SHARK

Length: up to 3.6m

This species can be found in the Atlantic, especially around the mouths of the Amazon and Zambezi rivers, and also in the freshwaters of Lake Nicaragua in Central America. It eats fish and squids, and has been known to attack and kill humans. There is a closely related species in the Indian Ocean, and in the River Ganges.

THE LITTLE HUNTERS

Sharks are a varied group of animals. Some are large and powerful hunters, but most are small and they feed off prey that is even smaller. Whatever their size, though, they are true sharks, hunting with the killer instinct. Some lay eggs, while others may give birth to live young.

MONKFISH

Length: about 1.8m

The Monkfish is the largest of a group of sharks called the angel sharks. They are halfway between sharks and rays, with bodies that are flattened when viewed from above. The Monkfish has sharply pointed teeth, and lives around Britain on the sea bed, eating shellfish, rays, and flatfish. They give birth to between 9 and 16 live young.

PYGMY SHARK
Length: up to 60cm

A rounded snout and large eyes are distinctive features of the Pygmy Shark, one of the smallest sharks of all. Because it finds its prey in waters at depths of around 1700m, where there is little light, the large eyes are important for its survival.

SANDY DOGFISH
Length: up to 75cm

This is a common shark round the coasts of Europe, including the Mediterranean. It can be found in large numbers in shallow waters, hunting along the sandy or gravelly sea bed for shellfish, small fish, and worms. Dogfishes are members of a group of sharks having a sharp spine on each of their dorsal (back) fins.

UNUSUAL SHARKS

Sharks have been swimming in the world's oceans for nearly 400 million years. Over that vast period of time, their shapes and features have changed considerably. The sharks shown here have evolved in unusual ways to fit in with their surroundings.

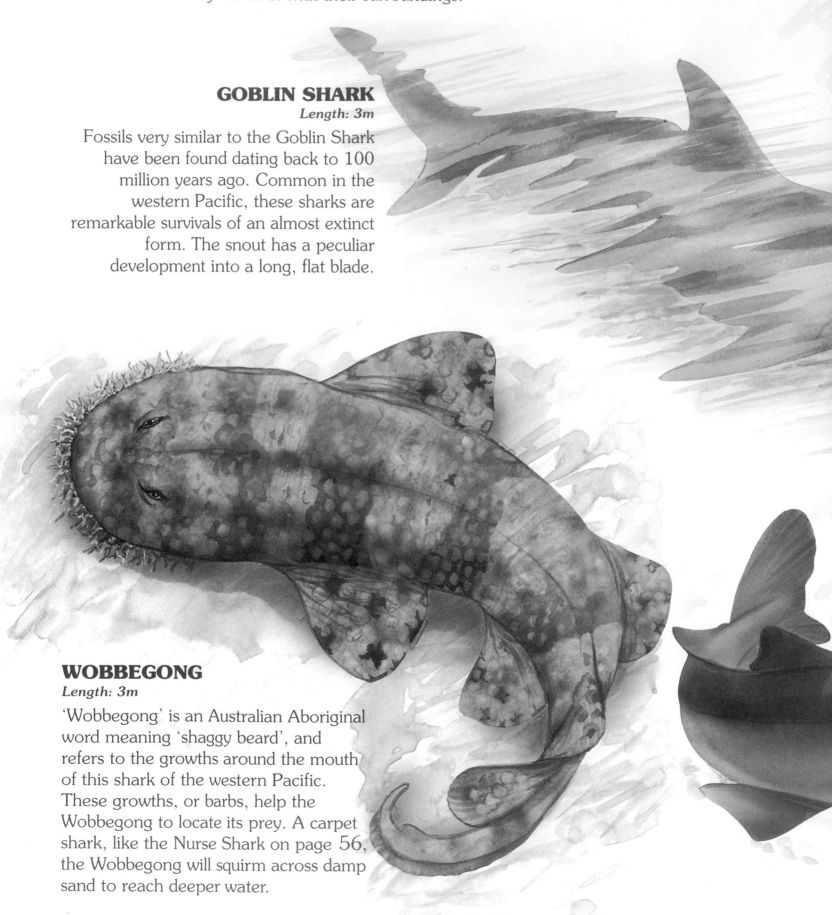

GOBLIN SHARK
Length: 3m

Fossils very similar to the Goblin Shark have been found dating back to 100 million years ago. Common in the western Pacific, these sharks are remarkable survivals of an almost extinct form. The snout has a peculiar development into a long, flat blade.

WOBBEGONG
Length: 3m

'Wobbegong' is an Australian Aboriginal word meaning 'shaggy beard', and refers to the growths around the mouth of this shark of the western Pacific. These growths, or barbs, help the Wobbegong to locate its prey. A carpet shark, like the Nurse Shark on page 56, the Wobbegong will squirm across damp sand to reach deeper water.

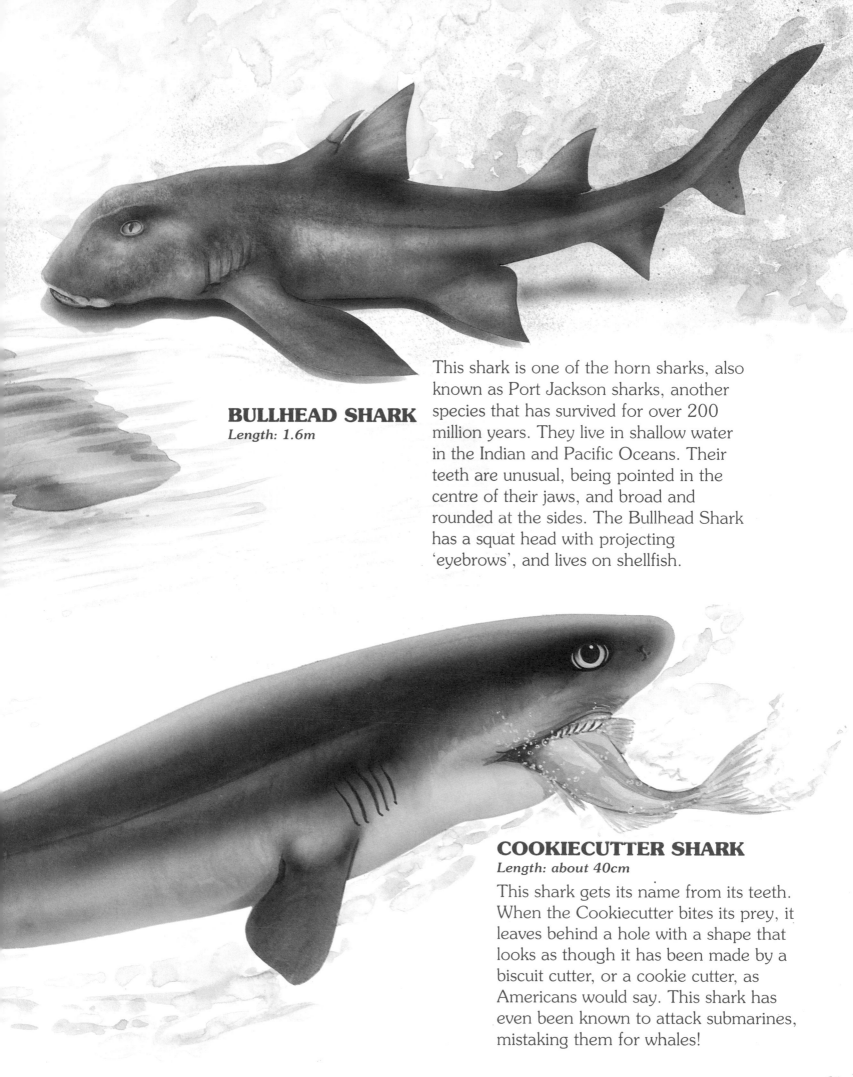

BULLHEAD SHARK
Length: 1.6m

This shark is one of the horn sharks, also known as Port Jackson sharks, another species that has survived for over 200 million years. They live in shallow water in the Indian and Pacific Oceans. Their teeth are unusual, being pointed in the centre of their jaws, and broad and rounded at the sides. The Bullhead Shark has a squat head with projecting 'eyebrows', and lives on shellfish.

COOKIECUTTER SHARK
Length: about 40cm

This shark gets its name from its teeth. When the Cookiecutter bites its prey, it leaves behind a hole with a shape that looks as though it has been made by a biscuit cutter, or a cookie cutter, as Americans would say. This shark has even been known to attack submarines, mistaking them for whales!

MAMMALS OF THE OCEAN DEPTHS

Whales are mammals which have adapted to life in the sea. In the distant past, when they were land-dwelling creatures, they had legs. In the course of time, the front legs have evolved to become flippers, and the back legs have disappeared completely. Whales breathe air, give birth to live young, and produce milk for their babies, or calves. They have horizontal tails. The Sperm Whales are those that have a reservoir of clear, waxy liquid, called spermaceti, in the nose. This adds buoyancy to the head, and makes deep diving easier.

GREAT SPERM WHALE
Length: up to 20m

The head of the Great Sperm Whale makes up one third of its body length, and much more than one third of its mass. The skin of an adult is patterned with circular marks, made by the suckers on the tentacles of the Giant Squid, with which the whale battles at depths of up to 3,000m! It finds its prey by echo-location. Because of man's hunting, this great whale is now quite rare.

PYGMY SPERM WHALE
Length: up to 3.4m

The Pygmy Sperm Whale is found in the warmer seas, and is smaller than some dolphins. It has a swollen nose, and a tiny jaw beneath its head. Slow-moving and deliberate in its movements, the Pygmy Sperm Whale is capable of diving to great depths in pursuit of squid and fish.

DWARF SPERM WHALE
Length: up to 2.7m

The smallest of the sperm whales is very shy, and, with its large, curved, back (or dorsal) fin, it has the profile of a shark. The rare Dwarf Sperm Whale lives in warm seas, and, like its huge relative, is able to dive deep and spend long periods underwater in search of its prey.

THE BIG-HEADS

There are three types of rare right whales in the seas today. The three species used to be numerous, but man has hunted them almost to extinction. They are slow-moving, and their bodies are so rich in oil that they float even when dead, so they were the 'right' whales to hunt! Right whales have no teeth. To feed, they draw huge amounts of water into their mouth, then filter out the plankton on which they live, through a series of horny plates, or baleen, that grow down from their upper jaw.

GREAT RIGHT WHALE
Length: up to 18m

This slow-moving whale can be found in shallow, coastal waters off a few parts of Canada, South America, South Africa, and in the Pacific. On the head, in front of the blowhole, there are crusted outgrowths, up to 10cm high, which are infested with barnacles, whale lice, and parasitic worms! The pattern of these growths is different for each whale.

BOWHEAD WHALE

Length: up to 20m

The largest of this group of whales, the
Bowhead Whale has an immense head,
taking up 40% of its total length. When
feeding, these whales swim along the
surface of the sea, mouths open,
gulping in great quantities of water, until
they have gathered enough plankton on
their plates of baleen to make it
worthwhile swallowing! Bowheads are
the only large whales regularly found in
the Arctic Ocean.

PYGMY RIGHT WHALE

Length: up to 6.4m

This is the smallest baleen whale, and
lives only around the Antarctic continent.
It is seldom seen, and is thought to be
very rare. Whales of this species swim in
an unusual way, moving the body up and
down in a wave-like motion.

THE GIANT WHALE

The largest whale of all, and, as far as we know, the largest creature ever to have lived on earth, is the Blue Whale, weighing up to 178,000kg. It is long and slender in build, with a powerful tail that can propel it through the water at up to 30kph. Blue Whales used to be found all over the world, but man has slaughtered them so ruthlessly that relatively few are left alive. Blue Whale calves are fed on milk by their mothers, about 600 litres a day! This milk is so rich, that a calf, which is born weighing around 7,250kg, will double its weight in one week!

BLUE WHALE
Length: up to 31m

When feeding, a Blue Whale will consume around 4 million shrimps each day! Most feeding takes place in the cold seas around the poles, while mating and breeding occur around the equator. Blue Whales can dive and remain under water for as long as half an hour. When they surface, they blow used air out of their blowhole to a height of up to 12m.

THE FAST WHALES

The fastest whales are all members of a group called rorquals, a word that comes from the old Norse for 'red whale'. In fact, rorquals are not red at all! The Blue Whale on the previous pages is a rorqual. With their long, slim, powerfully muscled bodies, they are capable of speeds of 30kph. In springtime, they move from warm to polar waters, where they can feed on the plentiful harvest of tiny shellfish, which they gulp down by the tonne. After being hunted almost to extinction, most rorquals are now protected.

HUMPBACK WHALE
Length: up to 17.5m

This whale is very different from the other rorquals. The Humpback Whale has numerous lumps around its jaws, each with a hair growing out of it. It also has two enormous flippers, about 5m long. During courtship, a pair of whales will rise together out of the water, clasping each other with these flippers, then crash back down again. Humpbacks produce the longest and most varied songs in the animal world. After being nearly wiped out, the few remaining Humpbacks are now protected.

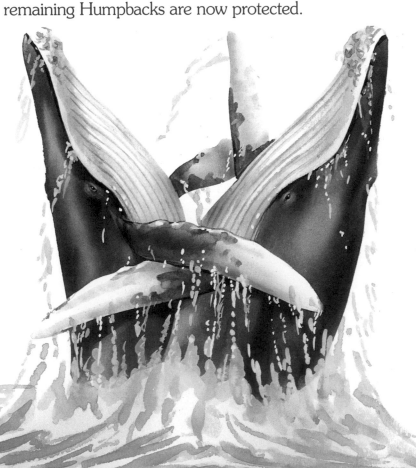

SEI WHALE
Length: up to 18.5m

The Sei Whale is distributed over all the world's oceans, except the very coldest. They eat about 900kg of food each day, plankton, fish, or squid, skimming them from the surface as they roll from side to side. Sei Whales are usually found in small family groups of four or five. Pairing is thought to take place for life. Sei Whales live for about 70 years.

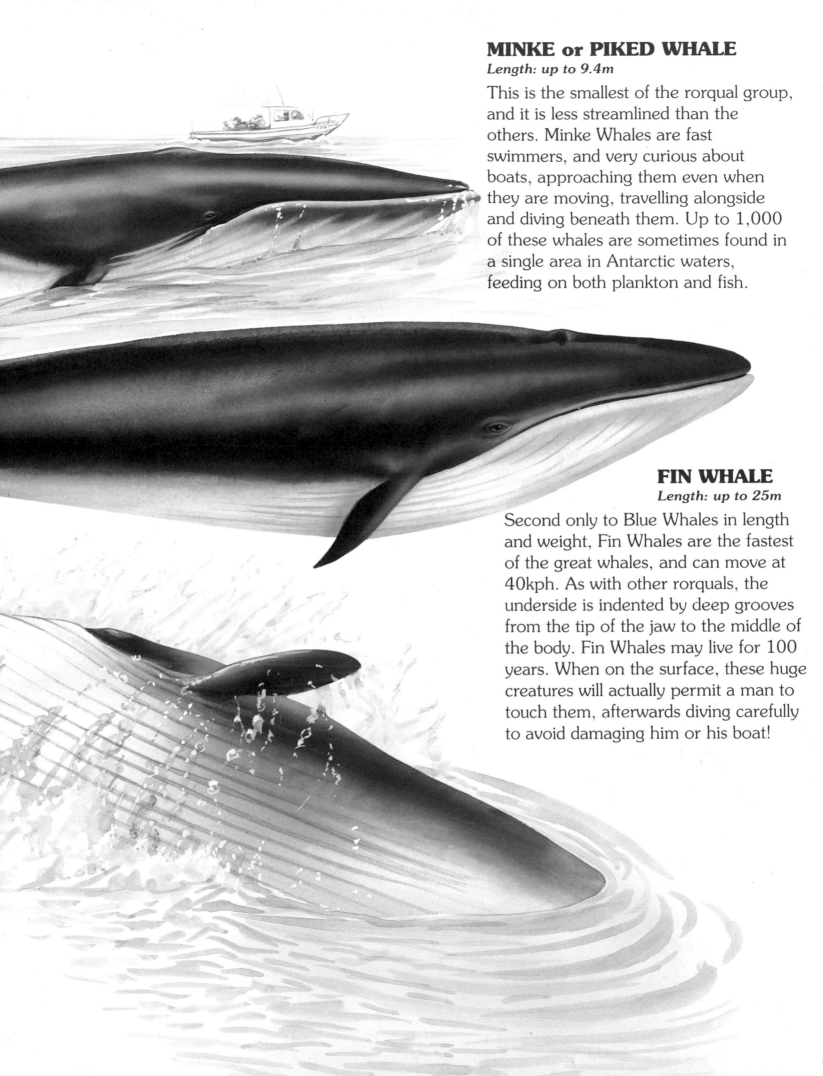

MINKE or PIKED WHALE
Length: up to 9.4m

This is the smallest of the rorqual group, and it is less streamlined than the others. Minke Whales are fast swimmers, and very curious about boats, approaching them even when they are moving, travelling alongside and diving beneath them. Up to 1,000 of these whales are sometimes found in a single area in Antarctic waters, feeding on both plankton and fish.

FIN WHALE
Length: up to 25m

Second only to Blue Whales in length and weight, Fin Whales are the fastest of the great whales, and can move at 40kph. As with other rorquals, the underside is indented by deep grooves from the tip of the jaw to the middle of the body. Fin Whales may live for 100 years. When on the surface, these huge creatures will actually permit a man to touch them, afterwards diving carefully to avoid damaging him or his boat!

'THE GREY SWIMMER ALONG ROCKY SHORES'

This was the name first given to the Grey Whale, by an American scientist, more than 200 years ago. This whale is in a species all on its own, somewhere between the right whales and the rorquals. We know more about the Grey Whale than we do about most, because there has been ample opportunity to study them on their mating and breeding grounds off the coasts of California. Grey Whales feed in the far northern seas, each year making the 20,000km trip south to California, the longest migration of any mammal, at speeds of 185km per day.

PACIFIC GREY WHALE
Length: up to 15.3m

Grey Whales feed on the Arctic sea bottom during the summer months. Little is eaten on the migration journey, nor at their destination. Calves are born exactly one year after mating, and the mothers and calves swim north again when the young ones are about two months old. Only when back in the Arctic will the mother break her 8-month fast! When a boat comes near, a Grey Whale will 'spy hop', or stick its head for about 2m out of the water to have a look at the intruder. They also 'breach', or throw themselves half out of the sea, many times in succession.

KILLER WHALES

There are three whales called 'killer', the Great Killer Whale, the False Killer Whale, and the Pygmy Killer Whale. Of these, only the Great Killer Whale really deserves the name, because it is a fierce predator. Even so, there is no record at all of any Killer Whale ever doing unprovoked harm to a human being. Remember this whenever you see a trainer in an oceanarium put their head into the mouth of a captive Killer Whale!

GREAT KILLER WHALE
Length: up to 9.75m

This streamlined whale has a heavy body, with large, paddle-shaped flippers, and a tall tail fin. It can swim at speeds of 50kph, and is to be found in all the world's open seas. They feed on a great variety of prey: squid, rays, sharks, seals, sea-lions, and other whales. One dead Killer Whale was found with 13 porpoises and 14 seals in its stomach! They live in family units of up to 50 members, working together to round up fish. Two Killer Whales have been seen tipping up an ice floe, so that a seal would slide off, into the mouth of another whale!

PLAYFUL DOLPHINS

There are many different types of dolphin in the oceans and rivers of the world. Here, and on the next two pages, we describe just a few of them. All small, toothed whales are sometimes referred to as dolphins, but the ones shown here are 'true', or beaked, dolphins. Dolphins have enchanted man from earliest times, with their intelligence, playfulness, and friendliness. They are famous for riding on the bow waves of ships.

COMMON DOLPHIN
Length: up to 2.6m

Common Dolphins are found everywhere, except in the coldest waters. In schools numbering hundreds, they can be seen leaping out of the water, catching flying fish in mid-air, and swimming at speeds of up to 64 kph. Dolphins will assist wounded companions and have even been known to help people in distress.

BLACKCHIN DOLPHIN
Length: up to 2.3m

Also known as Peale's Dolphin, after the first naturalist to identify it, the Blackchin Dolphin lives in small family groups around the southern coasts of South America. It is a friendly, little dolphin, feeding close inshore on fish, or on the seabed.

WHITEBEAK DOLPHIN

Length: up to 3.2m

This is the most northerly of dolphins, being the only species in the far North Atlantic. They eat squid, octopus, cod, and other fish. Whitebeak Dolphins will gather in schools of up to 1,500, all moving through the water together. It gets its name, of course, from its striking, pure-white beak.

BOTTLENOSE DOLPHIN

Length: up to 4.2m

Bottlenose Dolphins are familiar to us because of their appearances in films and on TV. In the wild, they are completely unafraid of people, approaching close to boats, riding on their bow waves, and rolling over to watch us watching them! They have the most amazing sonar system, and can even use it to distinguish between different types of metal. We need modern engineering instruments to do the same!

RIVER DOLPHINS

In some of the world's great rivers live dolphins that are very different from those in the sea. River dolphins are all small, with very long, narrow beaks. Because they live in muddy waters, their eyesight is generally poor, but they have remarkable echo-locating systems. By sending out loud clicks, and listening to the echoes, they can form a picture of their surroundings and locate their prey with complete accuracy.

GANGES RIVER DOLPHIN
Length: up to 2.45m

This dolphin lives in the great River Ganges, in India and Assam, from the mouth right up to the foothills of the Himalayas. Unlike other dolphins, this species swims on its side always, moving to an upright position only to breathe. Its slender beak can sometimes be 45cm long.

YANGTZE RIVER DOLPHIN
Length: up to 2.4m

In China, this dolphin is believed to be the reincarnation of a drowned princess! It lives in China's largest river, but, though it is protected, few are now left in the wild. Its beak turns up at the tip like a duck's. The Yangtze River Dolphin is a fish-eater, and very shy, staying well away from boats.

AMAZON RIVER DOLPHIN
Length: up to 2.7m

The colouring of this south American dolphin is an almost unbelievable, a shocking pink! Unlike its Asian relatives shown here, the Amazon River Dolphin has good eyesight, and will put its head out of the water to study a passing boat. It eats fish, including catfish and the fierce piranha. In the rainy season, these dolphins move into the flooded forests, but they always find their way back to the river when the water retreats in the drier weather.

HIGH-SPEED FISH

It is the speed of some fish that enables them to survive in the open seas. A few can power through the water at an amazing rate, far outstripping the fastest ship. High-speed fish have several features in common. Their bodies are streamlined, and muscular, and their tails are often large and pointed. These factors enable the fish to swim quickly, for long periods of time.

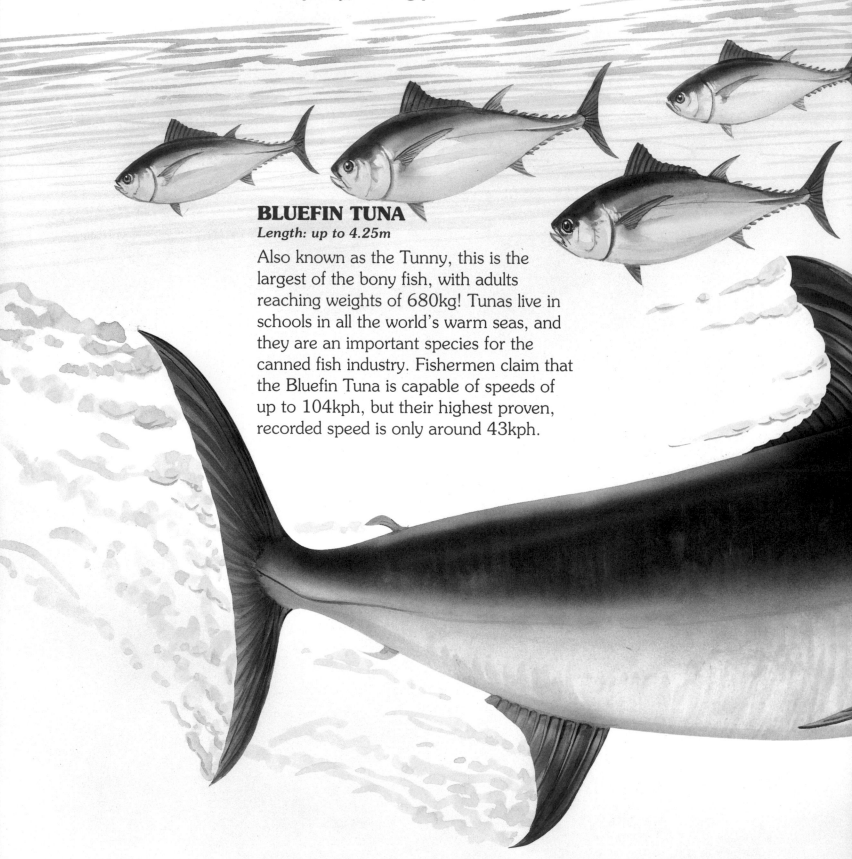

BLUEFIN TUNA
Length: up to 4.25m

Also known as the Tunny, this is the largest of the bony fish, with adults reaching weights of 680kg! Tunas live in schools in all the world's warm seas, and they are an important species for the canned fish industry. Fishermen claim that the Bluefin Tuna is capable of speeds of up to 104kph, but their highest proven, recorded speed is only around 43kph.

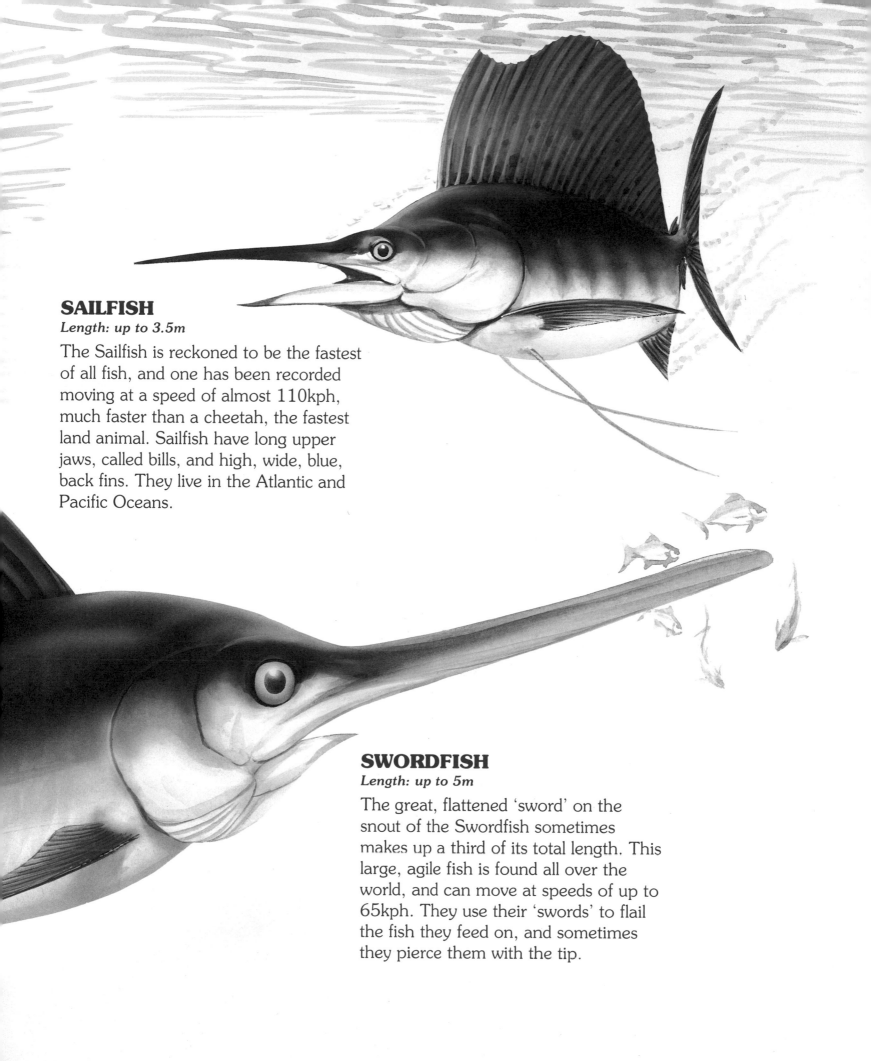

SAILFISH
Length: up to 3.5m

The Sailfish is reckoned to be the fastest of all fish, and one has been recorded moving at a speed of almost 110kph, much faster than a cheetah, the fastest land animal. Sailfish have long upper jaws, called bills, and high, wide, blue, back fins. They live in the Atlantic and Pacific Oceans.

SWORDFISH
Length: up to 5m

The great, flattened 'sword' on the snout of the Swordfish sometimes makes up a third of its total length. This large, agile fish is found all over the world, and can move at speeds of up to 65kph. They use their 'swords' to flail the fish they feed on, and sometimes they pierce them with the tip.

GRAPPLING GIANTS

Lurking in the ocean depths, there are a number of gigantic creatures which are rarely seen. In fact, science knows very little about these huge animals, except that they do exist. For centuries, they have featured in the stories told by sailors about their hazardous voyages.

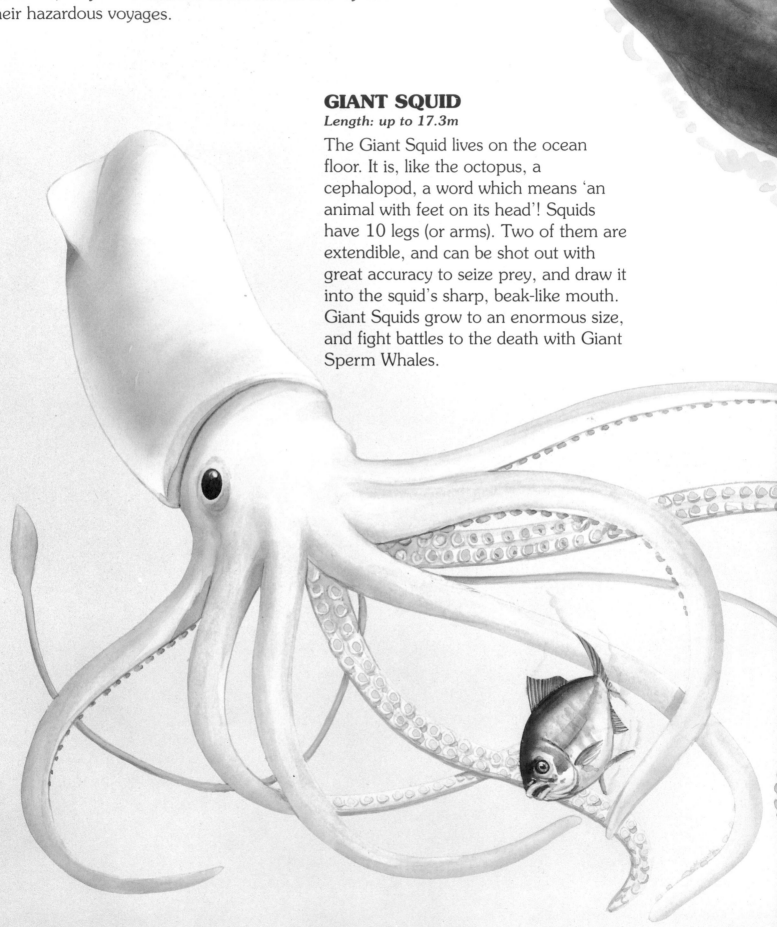

GIANT SQUID

Length: up to 17.3m

The Giant Squid lives on the ocean floor. It is, like the octopus, a cephalopod, a word which means 'an animal with feet on its head'! Squids have 10 legs (or arms). Two of them are extendible, and can be shot out with great accuracy to seize prey, and draw it into the squid's sharp, beak-like mouth. Giant Squids grow to an enormous size, and fight battles to the death with Giant Sperm Whales.

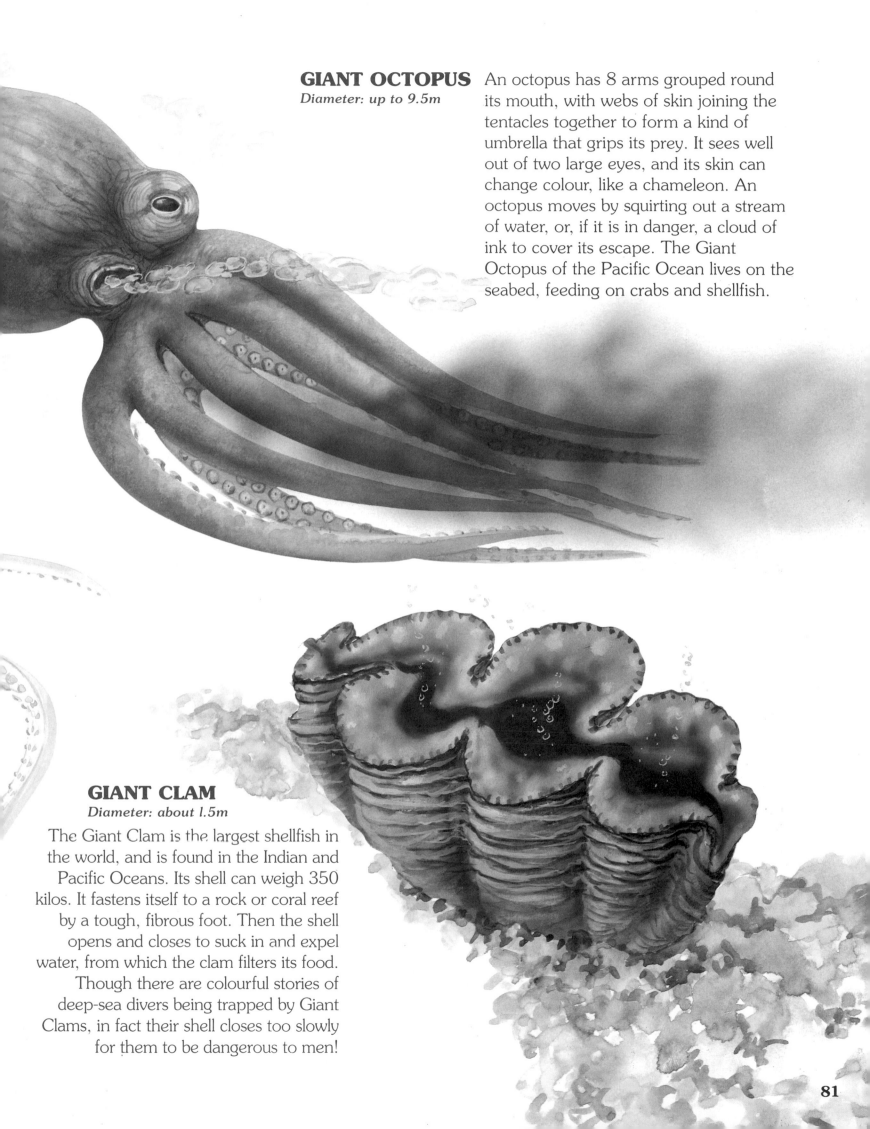

GIANT OCTOPUS
Diameter: up to 9.5m

An octopus has 8 arms grouped round its mouth, with webs of skin joining the tentacles together to form a kind of umbrella that grips its prey. It sees well out of two large eyes, and its skin can change colour, like a chameleon. An octopus moves by squirting out a stream of water, or, if it is in danger, a cloud of ink to cover its escape. The Giant Octopus of the Pacific Ocean lives on the seabed, feeding on crabs and shellfish.

GIANT CLAM
Diameter: about 1.5m

The Giant Clam is the largest shellfish in the world, and is found in the Indian and Pacific Oceans. Its shell can weigh 350 kilos. It fastens itself to a rock or coral reef by a tough, fibrous foot. Then the shell opens and closes to suck in and expel water, from which the clam filters its food.

Though there are colourful stories of deep-sea divers being trapped by Giant Clams, in fact their shell closes too slowly for them to be dangerous to men!

81

SNAPPING EELS

Eels are fish which have lost the fish-tail and most of their fins. Instead, their long bodies are very powerful, taking over the task of driving them through the water like snakes. All eels are hunters, attacking their prey on sight. They lay their eggs in deep waters, near the ocean bed, sometimes travelling thousands of kilometres in order to do this.

MORAY EEL

Length: up to 3.0m

Moray Eels are ferocious fish, with strong teeth, powerful jaws, and a savage bite. They live in cracks in rock or coral, or in wrecks, where they are safe from enemies. They wait for prey to come within reach, then dart out to seize it. Their fangs are poisonous in some species, and can cause a man's death. Skindivers must beware of them.

ELECTRIC EEL

Length: up to 2.4m

This is a freshwater eel of a different type to the others shown here. The Electric Eel is found in shallow streams on the Amazon and Orinoco Rivers in South America. Its body is lined with organs which generate a strong enough electrical charge to light a neon bulb. This charge will stun or kill any small animal within range, and even disable a man! The Electric Eel also finds both its way and its prey in muddy water by using its electrical charge as an echo-sounding device.

CONGER EEL

Length: up to 2.8m

This is another large eel with a mouth full of very sharp teeth. It can grow to over 45kg in weight. Conger Eels live in holes in rocks, harbour walls, and in wrecks, feeding on crabs, lobsters, and fish. Fishermen must handle Congers very carefully, and a large one pulled aboard a small boat is almost impossible to manage!

STRANGE NOSES

Some strange animals have developed in the seas as a consequence of evolution. Here we show some of the unusual noses which can be found, three fish and a mammal. Each nose serves a specific purpose for the species it belongs to.

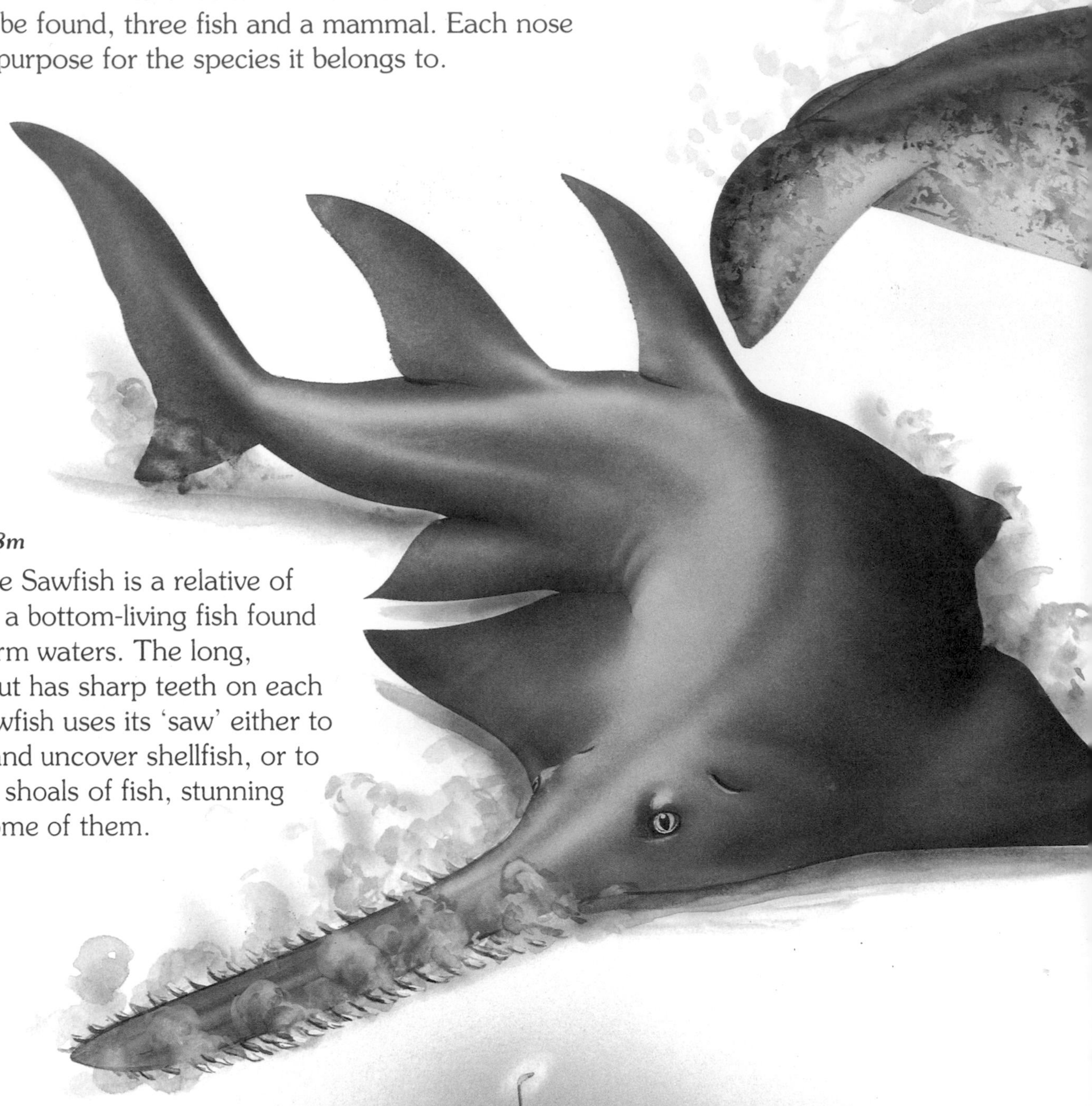

SAWFISH
Length: up to 8m

The shark-like Sawfish is a relative of the rays. It is a bottom-living fish found mostly in warm waters. The long, flattened snout has sharp teeth on each side. The Sawfish uses its 'saw' either to stir up mud and uncover shellfish, or to lash about in shoals of fish, stunning and killing some of them.

DEEP-SEA ANGLER
Length: from 15 to 120cm

The many different kinds of deep-sea angler-fish live at depths of from 100 to 2,000 metres. Shown here is one which has a 'club' with a luminous tip to it growing from its nose, just like an illuminated fishing-rod. In the murky depths, this glowing tip lures other fish within range of the deep-sea angler's large mouth full of razor-sharp teeth.

NARWHAL

Length: up to 6.2m

The adult male Narwhal or Unicorn Whale has an amazing spiral tooth growing out of its upper lip, forming a tusk of over 2.5m in length. This tusk is always worn smooth at the tip, since the Narwhal uses it to dig for food on the seabed. This mammal is found in small groups in the most northern waters, but is now rare, because too many are being killed by hunters...not for food, but to turn their tusks into souvenirs!

SAW SHARK

Length: about 1.4m

The small Saw Shark lives mainly in southern oceans. Its long pointed snout is bordered on each side with large, sharp teeth. These sluggish fish use their 'saw' to root around in sand and weeds, detecting food by means of sensitive barbs beneath their chin.

SIRENS, MERMAIDS AND SEA-COWS

In old legends of the sea, sirens and mermaids are beautiful women whose enchanted singing lures sailors to steer their ships to destruction on the rocks. Maybe the legend was first born when an ancient mariner saw a sea-cow bobbing on the surface of the sea, cradling its young one to its chest. In scientific language, the two species of sea-cow belong to a group called 'sirenians'. Sirenians are the only water-dwelling mammals to feed entirely on vegetation. The name 'sea-cow' comes from their habit of browsing, like a cow, on underwater grasses. Sea-cows are descended, in the far-distant past, from the same group of land-dwelling mammals as elephants!

MANATEE

Length: about 4.5m

Manatees are found along the east-coast of America, from Texas to the Amazon, and on the coast of West Africa. They are big, heavy animals, weighing up to 700kg, living in bays, inlets, and large rivers. Their paddle-like tail fin is nearly circular in shape. Both parents care for the young, with one holding it while the other dives for food.

DUGONG

Length: about 3.6m

The few remaining Dugongs can be found in the Red Sea, the Indian Ocean, or round Australia. These slow-moving, almost defenceless, mammals live in small groups, grazing on sea plants. They have a wide, forked, tail fin, and the males develop two tusks, about 25cm long. Dugongs are now rare, as men hunt them mercilessly, for their flesh, hides, oil, and tusks!

SEALS WITH EARS

There are two groups of seals with ears: the sea-lions, sometimes called hair seals, and the fur seals, sometimes called sea bears. Sea-lions have a coarse coat of hair only, while fur seals have a thick undercoat of fur beneath the hair. All seals, and the walrus, evolved from land mammals in the distant past, their legs having become flippers. When swimming, eared seals use their front limbs as oars. On land, they can walk in a clumsy way with the aid of all four flippers.

CALIFORNIAN SEA-LION
Length: up to 2.4m

The Californian Sea-lion lives in the Pacific, off the coasts of America, Korea, and Japan. It feeds on fish and squid, sometimes coming ashore to rest on rocky beaches and islands. Playful and agile, with a great sense of balance, the Californian Sea-lion is the one most often seen in captivity in zoos, and performing in circuses.

STELLER'S SEA-LION
Length: up to 3.5m

This is the largest sea-lion, weighing up to 1,100kg. It is found in the same areas as the Californian Sea-lion. In the mating season, thousands of Steller's Sea-lions gather in certain places, where the males fight each other to build up herds of females. Because of their weight, it is difficult for them to move about on land.

ALASKA or NORTHERN FUR SEAL
Length: up to 2.2m

This species migrates from the coasts of the Pacific Ocean to the waters of the Bering Sea for its mating season. There, on the icy Pribilof Islands, the males, the bull seals, fight to mark out territories, and gather the females into their harems. One bull seal may have a harem of up to 80 females. A female gives birth to one cub, a year after mating has taken place. This seal's fur is highly valued, by some people. Hunting is controlled to prevent the species from being wiped out.

SOUTHERN FUR SEAL
Length: up to 2.2m

The Southern Fur Seal is similar in size and appearance to the Northern Fur Seal, but its fur is not considered to be so valuable...except to the seal, of course! Nevertheless, it has been almost wiped out by hunters, and the remaining few are protected.

TRUE SEALS

Seals without ears are called true seals. Their rear limbs are swept back beside the tail, which propels them through the water with a side-to-side sweeping motion. They can only move on land by wriggling forward in a series of jerks. Although true seals have no external ears, they have fully functional inner ears, and acute hearing.

ELEPHANT SEAL

Length: up to 6.5m

This is the largest seal of all, and can weigh up to 3,500kg. It is found mainly in the Antarctic. Elephant Seals get their name from the fact that old males have a kind of 'trunk' on the front of the head, which becomes inflated when they are excited. They were hunted for oil, and the species was nearly wiped out, but they are now protected, and numbers are increasing.

COMMON or HARBOUR SEAL

Length: up to 2m

This seal is found all over the northern half of the world. Harbour Seals are slow breathers, and can remain underwater for long periods. They feed on shrimps and fish, and, in turn, they are preyed on by killer whales and polar bears.

HOODED SEAL

Length: about 3m

Hooded Seals are occasionally seen off the coasts of Britain or France. Living in the north Atlantic and Arctic Oceans, they spend most of their time out at sea, often on drifting icebergs. Adult males have a pouch of skin which reaches from their nostrils to the back of the head. When excited, the seal can blow air into this, so that it becomes like a hood or crest.

LEOPARD SEAL

Length: about 3.5m

The large, fast-swimming Leopard Seal lives in the most southerly seas, from the Antarctic ice to Australia. It feeds mainly on fish, but will also take penguins, and the young of other seal species. Like the leopard on land, the Leopard Seal is very aggressive, with powerful teeth.

THE WALRUS

The Walrus is halfway between a true seal and a sea-lion. Like a seal, the Walrus has no external ears. Like a sea-lion, the Walrus can use its back limbs for moving about on land. It differs from both groups in its teeth. The Walrus has two enormous, downward-pointing tusks, which in males can grow to lengths of 80cm, and in females 50cm. These tusks are sometimes employed as weapons, but more often they are used for scraping shellfish from the sea bottom. The Walrus also has a tough, bristly moustache on its upper lip and cheek pads.

WALRUS

Length: up to 4.8m

As they are not such strong swimmers as
sea-lions, Walruses spend most of their
time in shallow water, or on ice floes or
beaches, where they gather in herds of
about 100. They live in Arctic waters, and
follow the ice line, moving south in winter
and north in summer. A Walrus makes use
of its tusks to haul itself onto an ice floe.
Sadly, as usual, the Walrus has been
hunted mercilessly, and its numbers are
greatly reduced. Some countries now have
laws to protect the remaining population.

MONSTER RAYS

Rays are closely related to sharks. Neither sharks nor rays are bony fish, having, instead of bone, skeletons which are made of gristle, called cartilage, which is rubbery and not as hard as bone. Neither sharks nor rays have the swim bladders that fish have. A swim bladder is filled with air and helps a fish to stay afloat even when not moving. Sharks and rays have to keep swimming all the time, or they will sink! Shown here are two different rays that grow to 'monster' size.

MANTA RAY
Width: up to 7m

The Manta Ray is the largest ray, and lives all over the world in warm waters. It is also called the 'devil ray' or 'devilfish', because of the 'horns' on each side of its head. In fact, these are just flaps of flesh which channel fish into its broad mouth. Mantas are harmless to men, and they 'fly' through the water with flapping movements of their huge fins, or 'wings'. A Manta Ray can weigh up to 1,300kg, yet at times they will leap right out of the sea, for no apparent reason!

EAGLE RAY
Width: up to 4m

The Eagle Ray gets its name both from
the eagle-like appearance of its head
with its heavily-browed eyes, and from
its 'flight' through water, which has been
compared to the flight of an eagle
through the sky. Eagle Rays live in
warm waters, feeding on the seabed on
clams and oysters. It roots up these with
its snout, and, as a consequence, it is
also known as the 'cownose' ray! The
Eagle Ray has a long, whip-like tail,
which, in some varieties, has a
poisonous spine at the end of it.

HORSES AND PONIES

by Maureen Spurgeon
Illustrated by Robert Morton and George Fryer

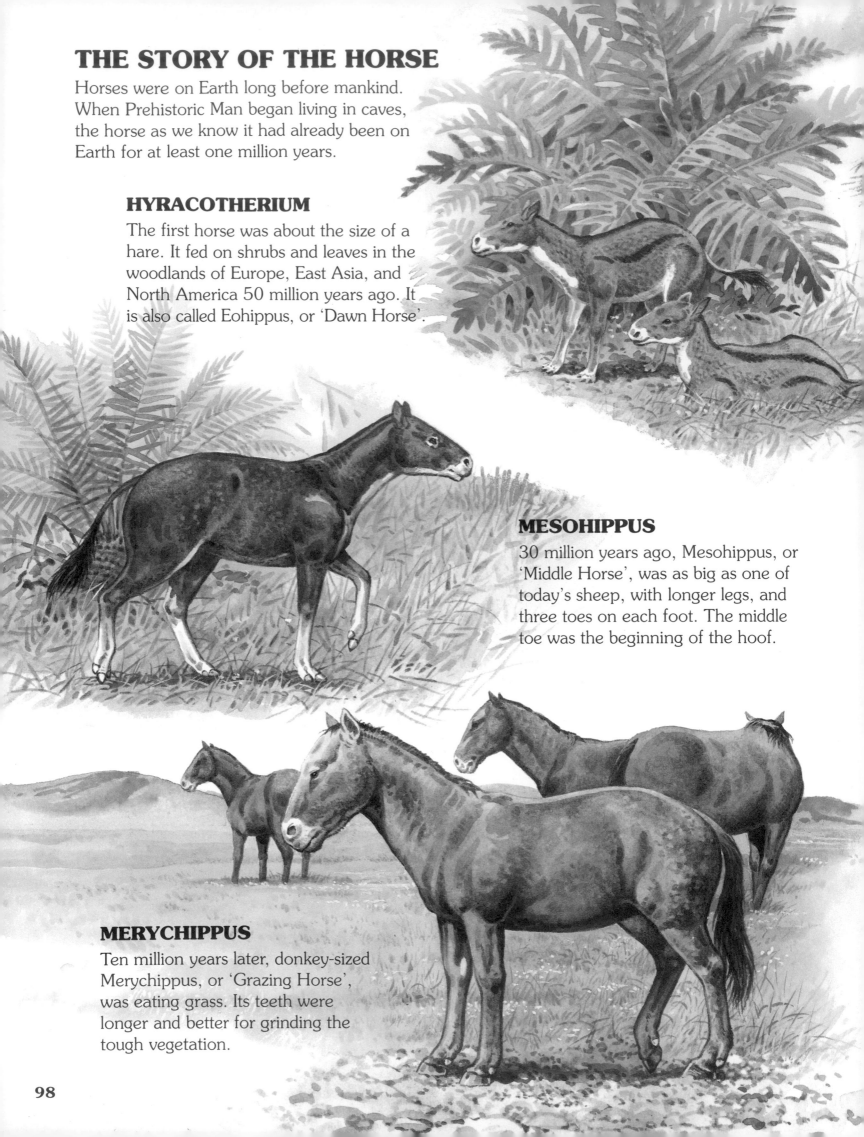

THE STORY OF THE HORSE

Horses were on Earth long before mankind.
When Prehistoric Man began living in caves,
the horse as we know it had already been on
Earth for at least one million years.

HYRACOTHERIUM

The first horse was about the size of a
hare. It fed on shrubs and leaves in the
woodlands of Europe, East Asia, and
North America 50 million years ago. It
is also called Eohippus, or 'Dawn Horse'.

MESOHIPPUS

30 million years ago, Mesohippus, or
'Middle Horse', was as big as one of
today's sheep, with longer legs, and
three toes on each foot. The middle
toe was the beginning of the hoof.

MERYCHIPPUS

Ten million years later, donkey-sized
Merychippus, or 'Grazing Horse',
was eating grass. Its teeth were
longer and better for grinding the
tough vegetation.

PLIOHIPPUS

Another ten million years later, and the horse was as big as a pony. It had hooves of a kind, and longer legs so that it could flee from danger and travel further for pasture.

EQUUS

With its toe bones fused together into a proper hoof, 'Modern Horse' began living on Earth about two million years ago. It has changed little since then.

TYPES OF HORSES

There are many *breeds* of horses, each distinguished by specific colourings and markings, as well as by size, character and body features. In addition, horses and ponies may be classified as various types.

HACK

A hack is a type of horse which is ridden purely for pleasure. Its neck and legs are long and elegant, and its lightweight body makes it the perfect horse for female riders.

EVENTER

An eventer is a horse of many talents! It has to compete in dressage (see pages 120-121), over cross-country courses, and at showjumping – the three sections which make up the competition known as an 'event'.

HUNTER

A hunter can be any horse which is suitable for fox-hunting, hence the name. But a person who is not interested in hunting may choose a hunter for its ability to carry a rider of any weight over any sort of country.

COB

A cob is a type of riding horse, often used for pulling wagons and carriages. Stout and strong, it has a short neck, and short, thick legs.

HORSES AND PONIES ON SHOW

Many horses and ponies love performing for a crowd! As well as for the characteristics of their particular breeds, they are chosen for their stamina, intelligence and obedience.

SHOWJUMPER

Showjumpers are always the lighter breeds of horse, chosen for their quick reactions and ability to work with a rider, as well as for their natural intelligence and talent for jumping.

SHOW PONY

Show ponies are often working ponies, too. 'On show', they may be judged simply as examples of their breed, or ridden over a course in competition with other ponies.

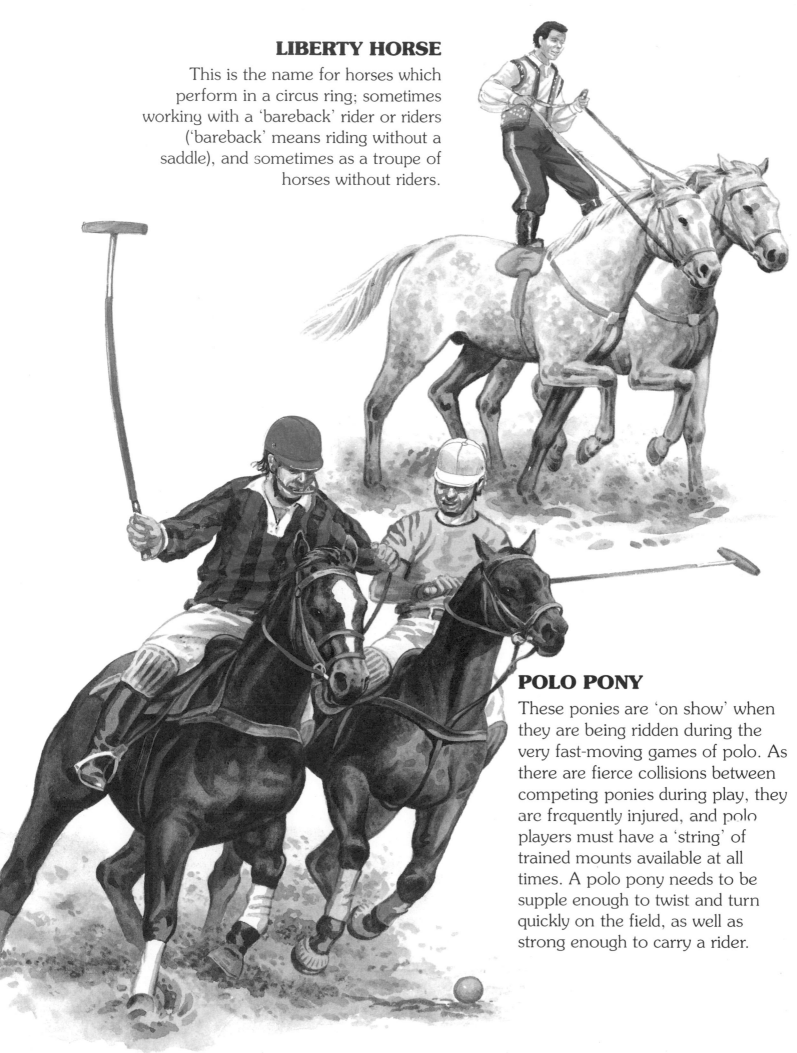

LIBERTY HORSE

This is the name for horses which perform in a circus ring; sometimes working with a 'bareback' rider or riders ('bareback' means riding without a saddle), and sometimes as a troupe of horses without riders.

POLO PONY

These ponies are 'on show' when they are being ridden during the very fast-moving games of polo. As there are fierce collisions between competing ponies during play, they are frequently injured, and polo players must have a 'string' of trained mounts available at all times. A polo pony needs to be supple enough to twist and turn quickly on the field, as well as strong enough to carry a rider.

BASIC TYPES . . . AND WILD HORSES

Today's horses have all developed from three basic, prehistoric types: the Steppe type (see Przewalski's Horse below); the Forest type, which is now extinct; and the Plateau type (see Tarpan below). Most of our finer-boned horses and ponies evolved from the Plateau type. Przewalski's Horse still lives and roams freely in the wild...just! The other 'wild' horses shown here are descended from horses that escaped from man in the past and became wild, or 'feralised'.

TARPAN

The Tarpan died out in the wild in Russia only 100 years ago. A few are still bred nowadays in captivity. The Tarpan is a descendant of the Plateau type of horse.

PRZEWALSKI'S HORSE

(Prish-voll-ski's)

Also called the Mongolian Wild Horse, or Asian Wild Horse, this was named after Colonel Nicolai Przewalski, who, in 1881, discovered a herd, unchanged since the Ice Age. A few, perhaps only 50 or so, still run wild in southwest Mongolia. This horse is a descendant of the prehistoric Steppe type.

BRUMBY

During the Australian Gold Rush in the 1850s, many farmers left home in search of their fortunes. The horses they abandoned became the first Brumbies, the wild horses of Australia. These were joined later by horses turned loose by the farmers who began using machinery, instead of horse power, after the First World War.

MUSTANG

When Hernando Cortez came from Spain to conquer Mexico in 1519, he brought horses with him. From these are descended the Mustangs of the American plains. Mustangs were often rounded up by cowboys for use as cow ponies. An untamed mustang was called a 'bronco'.

CLASSIC HORSES

Classic horses are those breeds which have influenced the breeding of horses throughout the world. Breeders and owners alike see in them the supreme standard of excellence by which to judge their own stocks.

ANDALUSIAN

The Andalusian horse comes from Spain. These great, white horses nearly died out after Napoleon's invasion of Spain in the early years of the last century. The breed was only preserved thanks to some Carthusian monks and a family called Zapata, who concealed a few pure-bred Andalusians from the French invaders.

BARB

The Barb is second only to the Arab as the oldest breed of horse. Pure-bred Barbs are very rare today, and are traditionally ridden by the Berber tribesmen of North Africa.

ARAB

The magnificent Arab horse can be traced back to around 3000BC in the deserts of the Yemen in Arabia. It is the oldest known, pure breed, and most modern breeds owe much of their development to Arab ancestors.

THOROUGHBRED

Although the Thoroughbred is descended from the Arab horse, it has long been regarded as a classic breed in its own right. Racehorses all over the world are from English Thoroughbred stock.

HORSES AROUND THE WORLD

There are many countries in the world which have at least one 'native' breed; that is to say, a breed that comes from just one particular place or area. Four such breeds are shown here.

APPALOOSA

This horse is easily recognised by the raised spots on its coat, especially on the hindquarters. Appaloosa is a corruption of 'Palouse', the name of a river in the American states of Washington, Idaho, and Oregon. The Nez Percé Indians of the region first developed the breed.

CAMARGUE

One of the most famous of all native breeds, the pale grey Camargue horses live in the swampy marshlands of the Rhône delta in southeast France. Now a recognised breed, its origins are shrouded in mystery.

HANOVERIAN

The Hanoverian owes much to the German-born British kings of the House of Hanover. Between 1714 and 1820, they sent the finest English Thoroughbreds back to Germany to breed with descendants of the German Great Horse. The result was the Hanoverian, which is one of the finest showjumping horses in the world today.

AMERICAN QUARTER HORSE

This horse was bred by early settlers in America, in Virginia and Carolina. It has become famous for its success over quarter-mile races (about 400m) – hence its unusual name.

PONY PARADE

When fully grown, ponies are small horses. Nearly all those
ridden today are descended from ponies which once roamed wild.

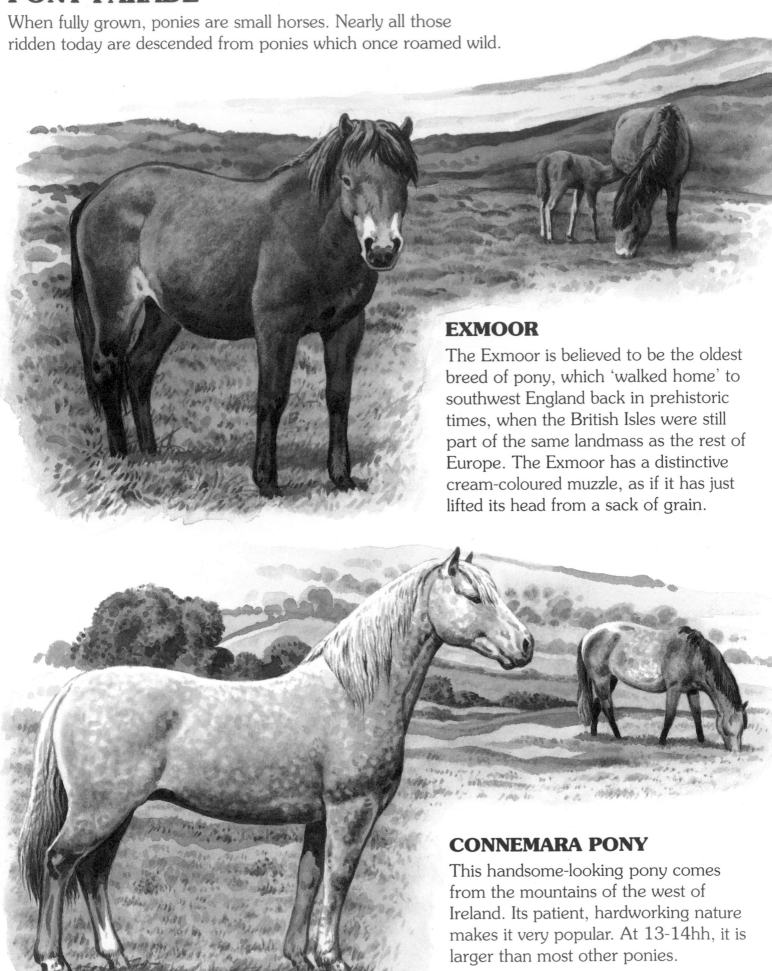

EXMOOR

The Exmoor is believed to be the oldest
breed of pony, which 'walked home' to
southwest England back in prehistoric
times, when the British Isles were still
part of the same landmass as the rest of
Europe. The Exmoor has a distinctive
cream-coloured muzzle, as if it has just
lifted its head from a sack of grain.

CONNEMARA PONY

This handsome-looking pony comes
from the mountains of the west of
Ireland. Its patient, hardworking nature
makes it very popular. At 13-14hh, it is
larger than most other ponies.

110

WELSH MOUNTAIN PONY

It is said that Julius Caesar began breeding the Welsh Mountain Pony after he invaded Britain. Strong and hardworking, it was widely used as a pit pony, and is now a popular riding and show pony.

SHETLAND PONY

At around 10hh, the Shetland is one of the smallest breeds, but also one of the strongest. It has a thick, woolly coat, a thick mane, a forelock falling across the eyes, and, most noticeable of all, a long tail sweeping the ground.

DARTMOOR

This close neighbour of the Exmoor is popular with young riders because of its kind nature and its intelligence. The Dartmoor pony is easily recognised by its long, shaggy mane and tail.

111

WORLD-FAMOUS PONIES

There are many breeds of ponies which come from different parts of the world – and many reasons why they have become famous in countries far from their native home.

FALABELLA

At just 7hh, the Falabella is the smallest horse in the world. It is named after the Falabella family, who began the breed in Argentina just over 100 years ago, developing it from the Shetland Pony.

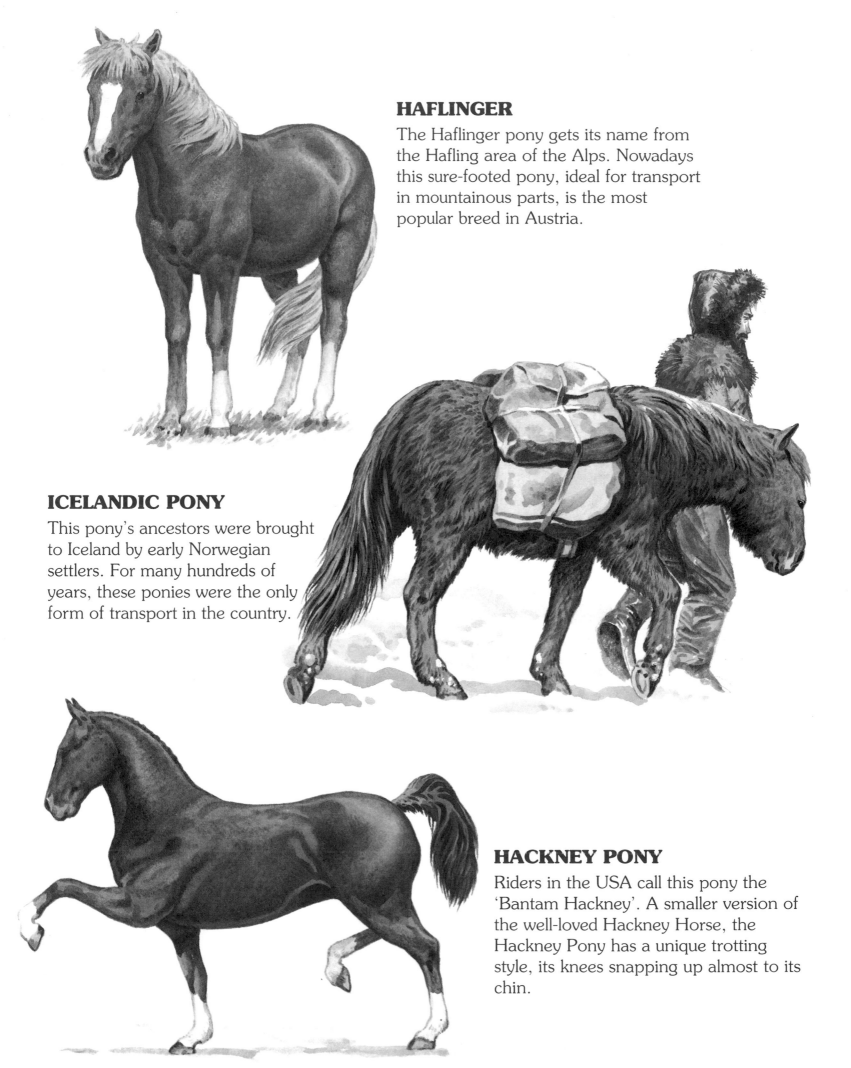

HAFLINGER

The Haflinger pony gets its name from the Hafling area of the Alps. Nowadays this sure-footed pony, ideal for transport in mountainous parts, is the most popular breed in Austria.

ICELANDIC PONY

This pony's ancestors were brought to Iceland by early Norwegian settlers. For many hundreds of years, these ponies were the only form of transport in the country.

HACKNEY PONY

Riders in the USA call this pony the 'Bantam Hackney'. A smaller version of the well-loved Hackney Horse, the Hackney Pony has a unique trotting style, its knees snapping up almost to its chin.

UNUSUAL HORSES

There are a number of very unusual horses throughout the world. Some are unusual because of their appearance, others because of their way of moving. Here are four of these 'unusual' breeds.

LUSITANO

This splendid-looking horse from Portugal is famous for its appearance in the bull-ring. In Portugal, bull-fighting is ceremonial and the bull is not harmed. The Lusitano is also used for farm-work throughout Spain and Portugal.

PINTO

The Spanish settlers in North America called this the 'Paint Horse' ('pinto' is Spanish for paint), which describes very well the horse's unusual piebald and skewbald colouring – as if its coat were splashed with paint.

KNABSTRUP

Denmark is the home of this unusual spotted horse. The Knabstrup has a long history as a circus horse.

PERUVIAN PASO

'Paso' is the Spanish for step, and it is the way the Peruvian Paso moves which makes it so unusual, flipping back its front legs, its rear legs sweeping forward in long strides. It is also called the Peruvian Stepping Horse.

HEAVY HORSES

There are 23 breeds of heavy horses throughout the world. Some of them are termed 'draught horses', meaning horses which pull a vehicle. Most were bred especially for farming, and heavy horses are still used for ploughing in many countries.

PERCHERON

This horse was first bred in La Perche in Normandy, France, about 130 years ago. It is well-known, throughout most of Europe, Canada and the USA, for its great strength and docile nature.

SUFFOLK PUNCH

The famous Suffolk Punch dates back to the Middle Ages, making it one of the oldest breeds of heavy horse in the world. Used for both draught work and ploughing, its colour is always referred to as 'chestnut', a special spelling of the word, just for this fine horse.

SHIRE HORSE

This is the most famous of heavy horses, popular all over the world. Placid and immensely strong, the Shire can pull weights of up to five tonnes. Whatever the body colour, all Shire Horses have white lower limbs and feet.

DUTCH HEAVY DRAUGHT

One of the largest of all heavy horses, with a massive, wide back and powerful limbs, the Dutch Heavy Draught is also one of the most recent breeds.

RACEHORSES

Horses have been raced for hundreds of years. Horse racing may have started for local amusement, but today it is both a sport and an industry, with classic horse races held all over the world.

HURDLES

Although hurdle racing began in Britain and Ireland, it is now popular in most parts of the world. Hurdles are 1.2 metres high, set out at four hurdles per kilometre.

FLAT RACING

In flat racing, horses race from 5 to 11 furlongs without jumps (a furlong is equivalent to 203 metres). Famous races include the English Derby, Australia's Melbourne Cup, and, in the USA, the Belmont Stakes.

TROTTING

Trotting races are seen in America, Australia, New Zealand, France, Italy, and in Russia, where they began. The horse is only permitted to trot, pulling a light, two-wheeled cart, called a 'sulky', in which the jockey is seated.

STEEPLECHASING

The steeplechase began as a cross-country race towards a church steeple, hence the name! Steeplechases are longer than flat races, with a set number of obstacles, including a water jump. Probably the world's most famous steeplechase is the Grand National, run each year at Aintree, near Liverpool, in England.

SHOWS AND COMPETITIONS

Horse shows and competitions are made up of different sections, like dressage and showjumping; and are of different kinds, like horse trials and gymkhanas.

SHOWJUMPING

Showjumping can take place inside a closed arena or out in the open. Apart from having a jumping ability, showjumpers have to be horses of speed.

HORSE TRIAL

As well as showjumping and dressage, horse trials include a cross-country event or steeplechase over fixed obstacles such as fences, hedges, and water hazards.

DRESSAGE

This is the most elegant of all competition events, in which rider and horse have to work together to achieve harmony in all movements, whether walking or trotting, coming to a halt, turning, or moving in a straight line.

GYMKHANA

A gymkhana is a competition for junior riders, and will usually include showjumping and novelty races.

THE HORSE AND FARMING

Before the arrival of the tractor, all farm haulage work was done by horses. In many parts of the world, farmers and growers still depend on the horse for their livelihood and survival.

HORSES AND CATTLE

Ever since men began herding cattle, horses have been used to round them up and to drive them. The most famous cattlemen are the cowboys of the USA and Mexico, and the Gauchos of Argentina in South America.

PACK-HORSES AND PONIES

These are the horses which carry heavy loads, particularly in mountainous regions where vehicles cannot go.

PLOUGHING

Many farmers still prefer to use heavy horses, such as the Shire and the Clydesdale, for ploughing, especially in rough or hilly areas where tractor driving is difficult.

HORSEWHEELS

In many parts of the world, teams of horses are still used to pull the wheels which provide power for mills to grind corn, or draw water from deep wells.

TRAVEL BY HORSE

For hundreds of years, ordinary people in many parts of the world depended on the horse for day-to-day travel.

TRAVEL BY BUS

Few motor cars were on the road when horse-drawn buses jostled for space with hackney carriages. These carriages were named after the Hackney Horses which pulled them, and were the forerunner of the taxi service.

124

TRAVEL BY COACH

Stagecoaches travelled from one town to another, picking up and setting down passengers. Only the richer people could afford this service, so highwaymen and outlaws soon saw an easy target in stagecoaches as they bumped over the rutted roads.

TRAVEL BY WAGON

For thousands of kilometres across North America, horses pulled the pioneer settlers in their covered wagons, which contained all their belongings, including the tools they needed to start a new life.

TRAVEL BY RAIL

To begin with, railway tracks were not laid for trains, but to enable horses to pull trucks and wagons along more easily. The first trams were also horse-drawn in this way.

HORSES AT WORK

Blacksmiths, or farriers, were once thought to have magic powers, because only they knew how to 'work' the iron for horseshoes. So they were always treated with respect, in case they had any magic to use against people they did not like! Few people could manage without the strength of a horse for long.

PULLING POWER

From coal wagons to dairy carts, from heavy brewers' drays to the barges which carried goods along the canals linking towns and cities, the horse once pulled them all.

POLICE HORSES

Police horses are useful for crowd control in many circumstances. From up in the saddle, police officers get a good view of what is happening.

PIT PONIES

Every coal mine once had pit ponies pulling heavily-loaded trucks underground. It is only in recent times that this labour has stopped, but ponies are still used in industry in some countries.

CARRIAGES AND COACHES

Many different types of carriages have been built worldwide, and some are used on state occasions even today. Carriage driving with teams of two or four horses is also an increasingly popular sport.

PERFORMING HORSES

There are few people who can resist the colour and spectacle of horses in a show. Sometimes, a horse is specially trained; at other times, the horse's performance is part of its nature; or it is really just doing a job of work.

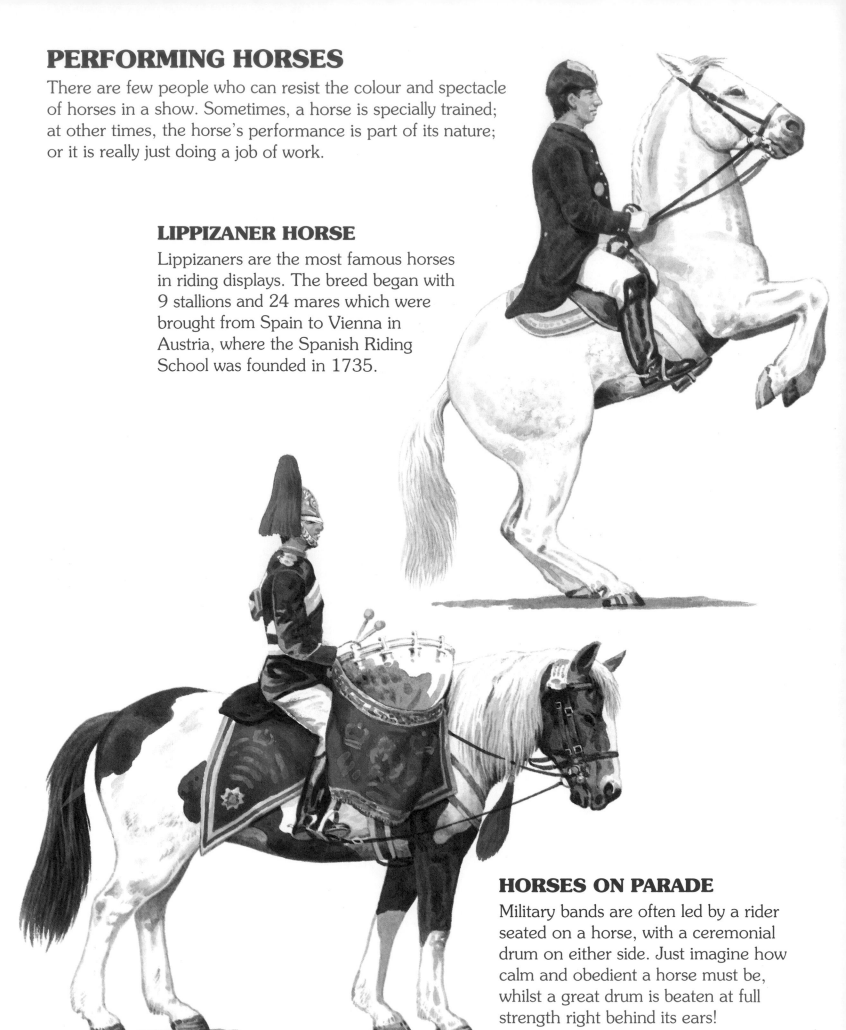

LIPPIZANER HORSE

Lippizaners are the most famous horses in riding displays. The breed began with 9 stallions and 24 mares which were brought from Spain to Vienna in Austria, where the Spanish Riding School was founded in 1735.

HORSES ON PARADE

Military bands are often led by a rider seated on a horse, with a ceremonial drum on either side. Just imagine how calm and obedient a horse must be, whilst a great drum is beaten at full strength right behind its ears!

RODEO

The rodeo is a show in which American cowboys demonstrate their skill in riding the 'bucking bronco', or unbroken (untamed) horse. A 'bronco-buster' is a cowboy who tames and rides wild broncos, or mustangs.

TACK

When horse people talk about tack, they mean all the items needed to keep a horse clean and fit for work. Riders and horse owners often refer to tack as 'saddlery', and, after riding, every piece has to be carefully cleaned and put away in a special place, usually called the 'tack room'.

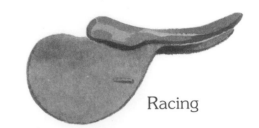

Racing

General

Jumping

Side-saddle

SADDLE

Different types of saddle include the lightweight racing saddle used by jockeys; side-saddles, which many female riders prefer; and the western saddle with the high 'pommel' in front, upon which a cowboy can keep a lasso. The most widely used is the general purpose saddle.

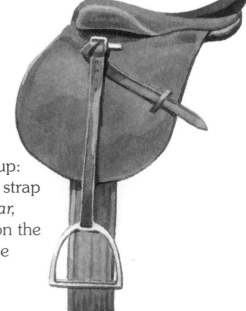

Western

STIRRUPS

There are three parts to each stirrup: the *Stirrup Leather*, an adjustable strap which goes through the *Stirrup Bar*, which is covered by the skirt flap on the saddle; and the *Stirrup Iron* for the rider's foot.

GIRTH

This is the long leather strap which goes under the horse's belly to hold the saddle firmly in place on the horse's back. The girth buckles on to the saddle, underneath the saddle flap.

BRIDLE

All types of bridle consist of the following: the *Headpiece,* going over the horse's head, behind its ears; the *Browband,* which goes in front of its ears; the *Noseband;* two *Cheek-Pieces,* to which the *Bit* is attached, which goes inside the horse's mouth, over its tongue; the *Reins* are attached to the Bit; and the *Throat Lash,* which buckles under the horse's throat to prevent the Bridle from slipping down over its ears.

CARE OF A HORSE

Almost everyone who is interested in horses has dreams of owning one. If you are ever lucky enough to see this dream coming true, do remember that, like any other animal, a horse takes a lot of looking after. Here are some important points to bear in mind.

GROOMING

It takes about half an hour to groom a horse before riding. Afterwards, a brisk rub-down will have to be followed by more grooming. Keeping a horse well-groomed and in good shape takes a great deal of time!

WHAT AGE?

Many ponies and horses are taken from their mothers far too early, making them nervous and difficult to handle. Riding a pony before it is three and a half to four years old could permanently damage its spine.

CHOOSING A HORSE OR PONY

Do go to a reputable stable – ask a local
veterinary surgery for a recommendation.
Then have a good look around to see
what the animals are like. Do they seem
contented and well looked after? Are the
stables clean, with good exercise space
for the horses? Do the horses seem
interested in their surroundings?

SPACE

Any horse must have space for exercise
as well as grazing. Even the tamest of
horses will quickly become bad-
tempered when it is cooped up for long
periods.

POINTS OF A HORSE

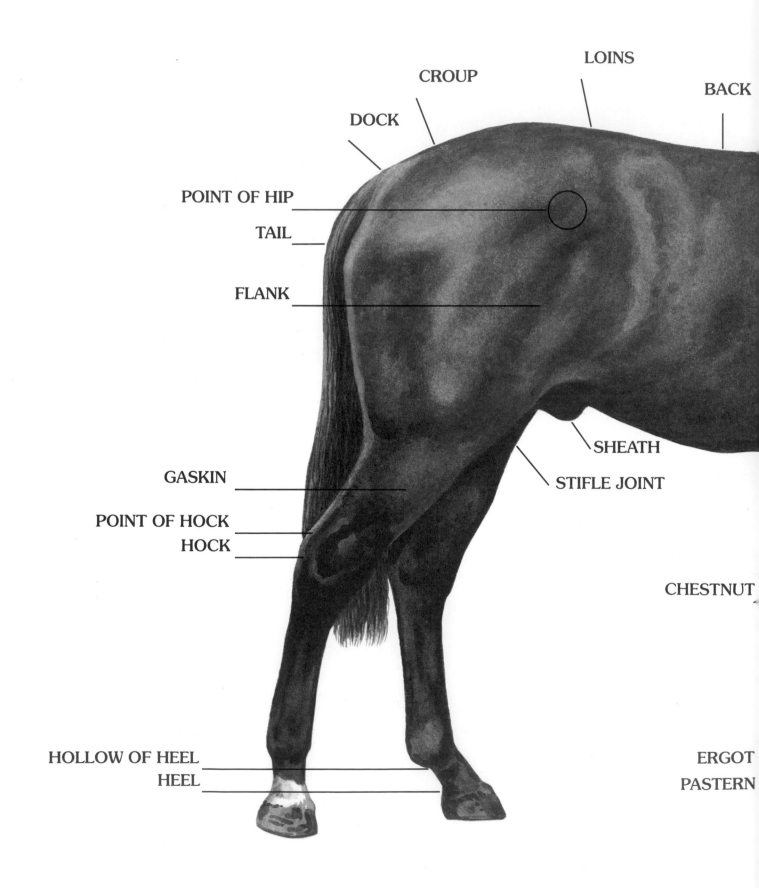

LOINS

CROUP

BACK

DOCK

POINT OF HIP

TAIL

FLANK

SHEATH

STIFLE JOINT

GASKIN

POINT OF HOCK

HOCK

CHESTNUT

HOLLOW OF HEEL

HEEL

ERGOT

PASTERN

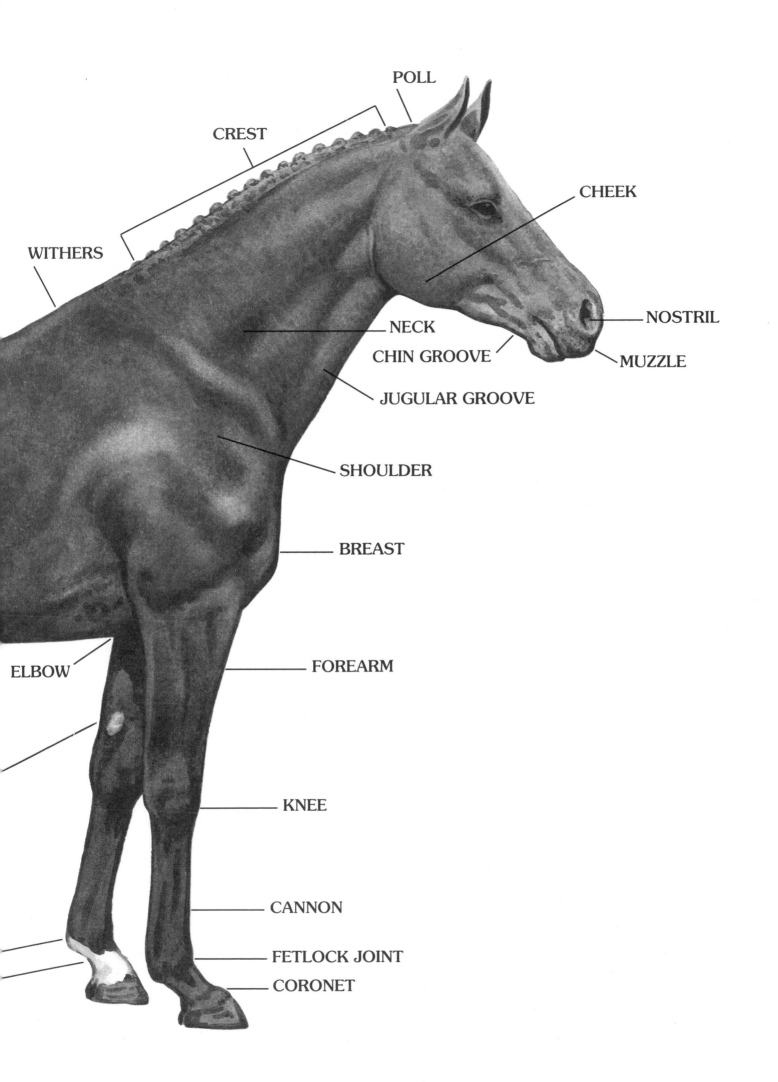

POLL

CREST

CHEEK

WITHERS

NOSTRIL

NECK

CHIN GROOVE

MUZZLE

JUGULAR GROOVE

SHOULDER

BREAST

ELBOW

FOREARM

KNEE

CANNON

FETLOCK JOINT

CORONET

ASSES, DONKEYS AND MULES

Although, perhaps, the most humble members of the horse family in terms of breeding, asses, donkeys and mules are the true 'beasts of burden', the working animals on whom the lives of people have depended for thousands of years.

ASS

Wild asses live in the deserts of northeast Africa. They are easily recognised by their long ears. The ass also has much smaller hooves than a horse.

ONAGER (or Asian Wild Ass)

Onagers can still be found in the wild, from the Middle East to the deserts of northwest India. Well over 2000 years ago, they were used for chariot racing, especially by the Assyrians.

MULE

Why is a Mule so strong? Because it gets its strength and toughness from its male donkey (jackass) father, and from its mare mother it inherits the size of a horse.

DONKEY

The Donkey is descended from the African Wild Ass. Being easier to keep and cheaper to feed than a horse, it is widely used in poor countries. Donkeys are also sure-footed, and so work well in rocky areas.

HORSES IN HISTORY

For many hundreds of years, until recent times, soldiers and explorers took horses with them wherever they went. The animals were often crowded together in ships and kept in terrible conditions below decks. Men always took more horses than they actually needed, knowing that many would not survive a long voyage. Untold numbers of horses have also perished alongside men in wars and battles throughout the course of history.

MONGOLS

In the 13th Century, led by Genghis Khan, the Mongols were among the finest horsemen ever known. After conquering a vast territory from China to Afghanistan, the Mongols moved into southeast Europe. Their empire extended from the Black Sea in the west to the Yellow Sea in the east.

THE CHARGE OF THE LIGHT BRIGADE

The Charge of the Light Brigade took place in 1854, during the Battle of Balaclava, in the Crimean War. Hundreds of cavalrymen and their horses were killed when the British Light Cavalry was ordered to charge the heavy cannons of the Russian Army.

KNIGHTS IN ARMOUR

The 12th Century Crusaders, in their 'holy war' on behalf of the Christian Church, were the first knights in armour. For centuries afterwards, throughout Europe, Asia, and North Africa, men wore armour in battle to protect both rider and horse.

CHARIOT RACING

Four-horse chariot races formed part of the Olympic Games in Greece in 7 BC. Centuries before that, the Ancient Romans had begun chariot racing around a special course called a 'hippodrome'.

HORSE FACT FILES

COLOUR TYPES

Palomino: coat; cream: mane, tail; fair almost white
Dun-Yellow Dun: coat; golden-yellow to cream
  -Blue Dun: coat; blue-grey
Bay: coat; brown: mane, tail; black
Chestnut: coat; reddish brown: mane, tail; lighter
Roan-Strawberry Roan: coat; mixed chestnut and white hairs
  -Blue Roan: coat; brown, some white

THE HORSE FAMILY

Stallion: male, age 4+, able to sire a foal
Mare: female, age 4+
Sire: father of foal
Dam: mother of foal
Foal: baby horse, up to 12 months
Colt: male, up to 4 yrs old
Filly: female, up to 4 yrs old
Yearling: colt or filly, 12-23 months
Gelding: male foal which has been gelded, or castrated, so unable to sire a foal

HOW MANY 'HANDS' HIGH

A horse is measured in 'hands', from feet to shoulders, or 'withers'. One hand is the width of an adult hand, about 10.16cm. So, if a horse is 15.3hh (hh=hands high), its height is 1.61m. 15hh would be a small horse. Ponies average about 12.2hh.

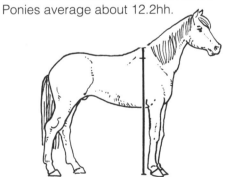

ARAB HORSE HISTORY

All English thoroughbreds, now racing worldwide, are descended from three individual Arab horses.
Byerley Turk: brought to England 1689 by Capt. Robert Byerley
Darley Arabian: brought to England 1704 by Thomas Darley
Godolphin Arabian: brought to England 1732

HORSES IN STORY AND LEGEND

Horses appear in stories and legends from many places.
Celtic Goddess, Epona, ruled over horses and ponies, often taking the form of a horse herself.
Norse God, Odin, rode across the sky on an eight-footed horse.
The Thracian Mares, in Greek legend, could run like the wind. They belonged to King Diomedes of Thrace, and were stolen by Hercules. All Greek and Turkish horses have ancient origins.
Pegasus, winged horse in Greek legend, was ridden by Bellerophon.

Black Bess, the legendary mount of English highwayman, Dick Turpin, was said to have been ridden by him over 300km non-stop from London to York.

PIEBALD AND SKEWBALD

These are particular types of colouring in horses and ponies.
Piebald: coat; spotted or patched, especially in black and white, in no particular pattern.
Skewbald: coat; irregular patches of white, or any colour except black.

PONY PENNING DAY

Only wild ponies live on tiny Assateague Island, off the coast of Virginia, USA. Nobody knows how they got there. It is thought their ancestors were being taken from Africa to America, when their ship was wrecked, and the ponies swam ashore to the island. Each year, in July, men from nearby Chincoteague Island take their own horses over to Assateague, to capture some wild ponies, and bring them back, amidst great excitement. This is Pony Penning Day.

UNUSUAL HORSE CUSTOMS

A horse's skull was often set into the topmost point of a Scandinavian house, to keep away ill-fortune.
An ancient cure for whooping cough was to let a piebald horse breathe on the sufferer. Many still believe a horse's breath is a cure for chest complaints.

LUCKY HORSESHOES

All horses need shoeing every 5-8 weeks, depending on their work and conditions underfoot.
For centuries, horseshoes have been symbols of good luck worldwide, because horses signified plenty, especially at harvest-time.
To 'keep good luck in', a horseshoe must be hung with its open part up.

RACING FACTS

Point-to-Point: Shares common origin with steeplechase; first race run across country from one 'point' to another. Now raced on a spectator course.
Most Famous Flat Race Ever: Probably the English Derby of June 1867. The winner *Hermit* had previously been near death, and a jockey was only found at the last minute.

Pages 120-121: Shows and Competitions
HORSES AND JUMPING

Horses and ponies are *not* natural jumpers, though most will usually clear a fence when they have to. For the show ring, they have to be specially trained, long before carrying a rider. All wear 'over-reach' bands on the front fetlocks to protect them from being struck during jumping by the hind shoes.

Pages 122-123: The Horse and Farming
HORSE POWER

An engine's strength is expressed as a measure of the pulling power of a horse. Horsepower is part of the specification of any vehicle.
Saddle Horses: These are horses that work on cattle stations, or ranches. The Australian Stock Horse, based on the Waler, is a famous breed of saddle horse.

Pages 124-125: Travel by Horse
STRAIGHT FROM THE HORSE'S MOUTH

Before telegraph cables and phone lines, news was carried by riders on horseback, or by coach. Along stagecoach routes, coaching inns were also postal stations, where letters and goods could be left, to be taken onwards by coach.
Pony Express: Briefly, in America in the mid-1800s, this was a fast postal service between Missouri and California.

Pages 126-127: Horses at Work
WORKING FACTS

Tow Paths: Paths beside rivers and canals, along which horses would trudge, towing barges.
Cock Horse: If a load was too heavy for a team of horses, especially going uphill, an extra horse, called a 'cock horse' or 'trace horse', was harnessed to the front.

Pages 128-129: Performing Horses
ON THEIR BEST BEHAVIOUR

Rodeo: Began as riding or roping contests between cowboys taking part in horse or cattle round-ups. Before branding, animals were held in enclosure called a 'rodeo', so contests became known as rodeos. During a round-up, cowboys relied fully on the skill and obedience of their well-trained cow ponies.
Drumming up Support: Phrase comes from army tradition of drummer on horseback urging soldiers on during a battle.

Pages 130-131: Tack
GROOMING

Grooming Kit: Kept in 'Tack Room'.
Brushes -Dandy: Removes heavy dirt.
 -Body: Brushes dirt and dust from coat, mane, and tail.
 -Wet: For mane, tail, feet.
Curry Comb: Mainly for cleaning the Body Brush.
Hoof Pick: Removes dirt or stones from hoofs.

Pages 132-133: Care of a Horse
MONEY IS NEEDED FOR . . .

Winter Feed: Hay and fodder.
Winter Stabling: If needed.
Vets' Fees: Healthiest horse needs the vet at least once a year!
Blacksmith's Fees: Horses need shoeing at least every 6 weeks.
Insurance: For horse, and in case it damages someone's property.
Tack: Saddle, bridle, reins, etc.
Riding Hat and Boots
PLUS entry fees for competitions, etc; loose boxes; jodhpurs and jacket, if you are competing!

Pages 134-135: Points of a Horse
PHYSICAL FACTS

Feathering: Shaggy tuft of hair growing behind fetlock, and usually hanging down over hoof. Shire Horses and Shetland Ponies are breeds with feathering.
Blaze: Broad, white marking between eyes, running all down face.
Teeth: As it ages, horse's teeth change in shape and size, which is how you can tell its age. Most easily seen is way that gums shrink back as horse gets older, making teeth seem longer. That is why, when someone gets older, we say they are 'long in the tooth'!

Pages 136-137: Asses, Donkeys and Mules
MULES AND HINNIES

Mules: Sterile, cannot produce young, not amongst themselves, nor with horses.
Hinnies: Offspring of 'jenny', a female donkey, and male horse. Hinnies are rarer than mules.
Both have reputation for being stubborn, but are brave and hard-working.

Pages 138-139: Horses in History
WARS AND WEALTH

Bucephalus: Alexander the Great's black stallion. Carried Alexander during conquest of Asia Minor, Persia (now Iran), and to India, an immense journey even by modern transport. Horse died in 326BC after battle on Hydaspes River. Alexander founded city of Bucephala in horse's honour.
Marengo: Grey Arab pony, Napoleon's favourite. He rode it throughout Battle of Waterloo in 1815.
Cavalry Horses: Ridden in battle until very recent times. Word 'cavalry' of French origin; they are the 'horse soldiers'.
Waler: Finest cavalry horse of World War I; from New South Wales in Australia.
Ponies and Mules: In World War II, used in Africa, Italy, and Burma to carry ammunition and supplies through mountainous regions.
Richest Horse in History: Probably *Incitatus*, favourite of Roman emperor Caligula (AD12-41). He showered riches on horse, including marble stall; solid gold pail, for water; manger carved from ivory. Caligula also made *Incitatus* a Roman Citizen and a Senator!

ANIMALS
Birds, Reptiles and Insects

by Colin Clark

LITTLE ANIMALS: INSECTS

Around a million different kinds of insects have been discovered so far, making them the largest and most varied form of animal life. There could be another 30 million varieties to be discovered! Insects are small creatures, with bodies divided into three parts, each part with a pair of legs. They live everywhere, though there are very few in the sea.

LOCUST

Length: 5–7cm

The locust is the largest of the grasshoppers. The Migratory Locust is a fearsome pest in many places, destroying crops and natural vegetation. So many swarm together and migrate that the sky becomes dark. About 120 years ago in America, a swarm of Rocky Mountain Locusts (a species that has since died out) was estimated as covering over 250,000 sq km, and took five days to pass over someone on the ground!

TERMITE

Length: 2cm

Like ants, termites live in large, underground colonies, or tall, mud towers, so strong that it has taken explosives to destroy them! One termite mound was found to be nearly 9m high! Sometimes called 'white ants', termites are actually more closely related to cockroaches. When one termite species marches through the African forest, the sound of millions of their heads striking the ground can be heard from many kilometres away.

BEETLE
Length: 0.5mm–19cm

With about 250,000 different species, beetles are the largest group of insects. All have biting mouths, and tough, horny, front wings, which cover and protect the delicate rear wings that are used for flying. The Hercules Beetle shown here is one of the largest, though its horn accounts for more than half its length.

HONEY BEE
Length: 1.2–1.8cm

Like all bees, Honey Bees have stocky, hairy bodies. They are social insects, with up to 50,000 living together in a colony. In the wild, they build their wax nests in hollow trees. Man-made beehives are accepted as just another kind of hollow tree! It is the worker bees who fly from flower to flower, collecting pollen (on their body hairs) and eating nectar (from which honey is made). In flight, their wings move up and down more than 200 times a second, and they may travel over 90km in a day.

DRAGONFLY
Wingspan: 10.6cm

Like other dragonflies, the Emperor Dragonfly flies very fast. Its eyes cover most of its head, enabling it to spot and catch other insects in flight. Dragonfly eggs are scattered into water or laid on underwater plants. From an egg, a nymph (an insect in the feeding and growth stages of development) is hatched. When ready, it climbs up a plant out of the water, where its skin splits open and the young dragonfly emerges.

145

OTHER 'CREEPY-CRAWLIES'

Insects are not the only strange-looking, small forms of animal life that we are likely to see scuttling around, though they are the most numerous. Insects are called *arthropods*, a word of Greek origin meaning that they have jointed feet. The animals shown here are also arthropods, but they are certainly not insects!

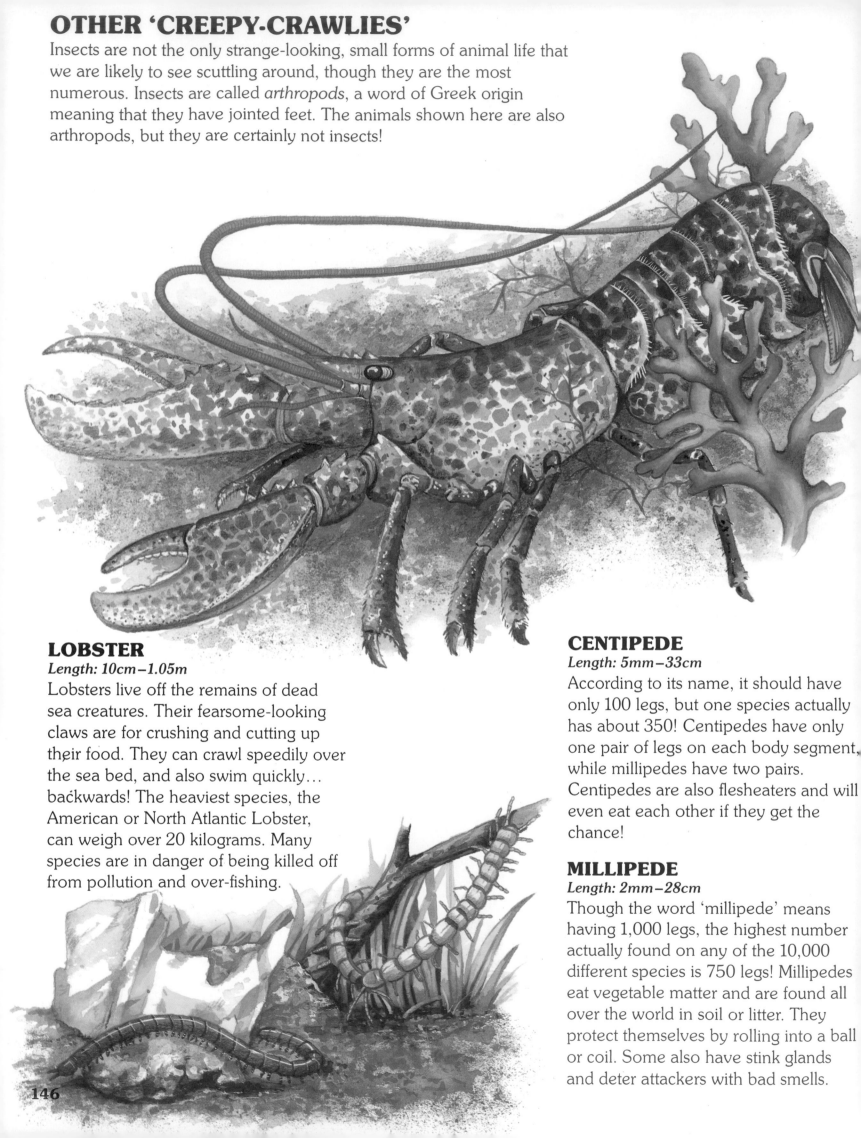

LOBSTER
Length: 10cm – 1.05m

Lobsters live off the remains of dead sea creatures. Their fearsome-looking claws are for crushing and cutting up their food. They can crawl speedily over the sea bed, and also swim quickly… backwards! The heaviest species, the American or North Atlantic Lobster, can weigh over 20 kilograms. Many species are in danger of being killed off from pollution and over-fishing.

CENTIPEDE
Length: 5mm – 33cm

According to its name, it should have only 100 legs, but one species actually has about 350! Centipedes have only one pair of legs on each body segment, while millipedes have two pairs. Centipedes are also flesheaters and will even eat each other if they get the chance!

MILLIPEDE
Length: 2mm – 28cm

Though the word 'millipede' means having 1,000 legs, the highest number actually found on any of the 10,000 different species is 750 legs! Millipedes eat vegetable matter and are found all over the world in soil or litter. They protect themselves by rolling into a ball or coil. Some also have stink glands and deter attackers with bad smells.

SPIDER
Leg span: 0.4mm – 26.6cm
Insects have six legs, spiders have eight. Their bodies are in two parts only. All have fangs which inject poison into their prey, but only about 30 kinds are dangerous to humans. Most deadly are the Brazilian Wandering Spiders, which enter houses and hide in clothes! All spiders produce silk, though not all make webs. For a large web, a spider might use 30 metres of silk!

SCORPION
Length: 1.0mm – 18cm
Scorpions are in the same family as spiders. They are found mostly in hot, dry places, feeding at night on insects and other small animals. They have large pincers, and a long, curved tail with a sting at the tip. Most are not dangerous to man, but the poison from the sting of one scorpion in the Sahara can kill in six hours!

CRAB

Shell diameter: 6.3mm – 28cm approx.
Crabs, like lobsters, shrimps, wood-lice, and water-fleas, are crustaceans, which means that they have shells. Most, though not all, live in water. They have five pairs of legs, the front pair ending in large claws, or pincers, which are used for capturing food, fighting, and signalling. They walk sideways, and their moveable eyes are on the end of stalks.

147

BREATHING UNDER WATER: FISH

Fish are cold-blooded animals with backbones that live all their lives in water, breathing oxygen from it through their gills. There are over 20,000 species of fish, most living in saltwater. About a third live in freshwater. As you can see from the examples shown here, fish come in all shapes and sizes.

ELECTRIC EEL

Length: up to 2.4m

This large freshwater fish lives in South America, in the Amazon and Orinoco Rivers. It generates an electric shock of over 500 volts, strong enough to disable a man. It uses this power to kill its prey, and as a defence. Since it lives in very dark waters, the Electric Eel also 'bounces' electrical pulses off its surroundings as an aid to navigation.

FLATFISH

Length: 120mm – 2.4m

We eat many kinds of flatfish, like Halibut, Sole, and Plaice. When they hatch from eggs, flatfish have an eye on each side of their mouths. As they grow, one side of the body becomes coloured to match the sea bottom where they feed, and one eye moves round to join the other on the coloured side. The 'blind side' remains colourless. Strangely, each flatfish species consistently has eyes to one particular side of the mouth. Turbots' eyes are always to the right; halibuts' to the left.

SEAHORSE

Length: up to 30cm

The seahorse is a 'tube-mouth' fish, meaning it has a long, tube-like snout, which gives it its unique, horse-like head. It swims upright in the water. For about five weeks after the female has laid her eggs, they are carried by the male seahorse in a special pouch, until they hatch out as miniature versions of the adults.

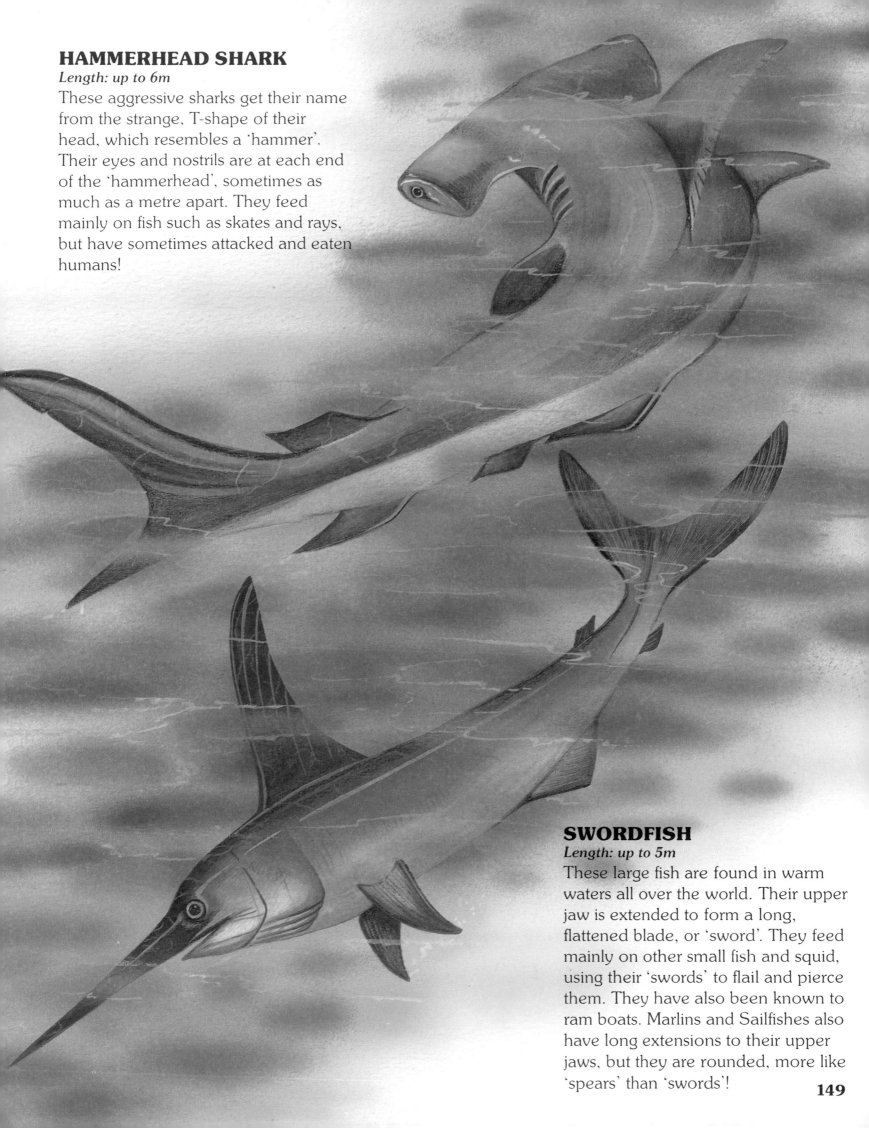

HAMMERHEAD SHARK

Length: up to 6m

These aggressive sharks get their name from the strange, T-shape of their head, which resembles a 'hammer'. Their eyes and nostrils are at each end of the 'hammerhead', sometimes as much as a metre apart. They feed mainly on fish such as skates and rays, but have sometimes attacked and eaten humans!

SWORDFISH

Length: up to 5m

These large fish are found in warm waters all over the world. Their upper jaw is extended to form a long, flattened blade, or 'sword'. They feed mainly on other small fish and squid, using their 'swords' to flail and pierce them. They have also been known to ram boats. Marlins and Sailfishes also have long extensions to their upper jaws, but they are rounded, more like 'spears' than 'swords'!

149

BETWEEN FISH AND REPTILES: AMPHIBIANS

The cold-blooded amphibians are really halfway between fish and reptiles. Most spend the first part of their lives in water, moving onto land as they become adults. They are found close to freshwater, or in wet places, but no amphibians live in the sea. There are about 4,000 different species in the world.

FROG

Length: 12mm–36.8cm

To scientists, both frogs and toads are classified within the same group of amphibians without tails. The only difference is that frogs have smooth, wet skin, while toads have rough, dry skin. Frogs are found everywhere in the world, except the Arctic and Antarctic. The strongest known poison comes from the skin of the Golden Poison-Dart Frog in South America. One frog has enough poison to kill 1,500 people!

TOAD

Length: under 24mm–over 24cm

Toads are able to exist at higher altitudes than frogs. One has even been found in the Himalayas at a height of 8,000 metres. It can also be dangerous to touch their skin, because they can give off a whitish fluid which can cause severe burning to a person's eyes or mouth. As with frogs, they lay their eggs in water, where they hatch into tadpoles, which later move onto land to become adult toads.

SALAMANDER and NEWT

Length: under 15mm–1.8m

Salamanders and newts are amphibians with tails. Salamanders look like lizards, which are reptiles, but salamanders have no claws, nor scales on their bodies. Most are active only at night, avoiding direct light. Some species, like the Olm, in Europe, live in underground streams and caves, and are completely blind. If a salamander loses a leg or its tail, it can grow a new one! Newts are familiar sights in garden ponds. Some are brightly coloured and have a crest running down their back.

CAECILIAN

pronounced 'SEE-sill-yan'
Length: 10cm–1.4m

The Caecilians are blind amphibians *without legs*! They look rather like worms with jaws and teeth. They live in swamps or in streams in tropical parts of the world, but since they are very difficult to find even when you are looking for them, you probably will never see one in the wild!

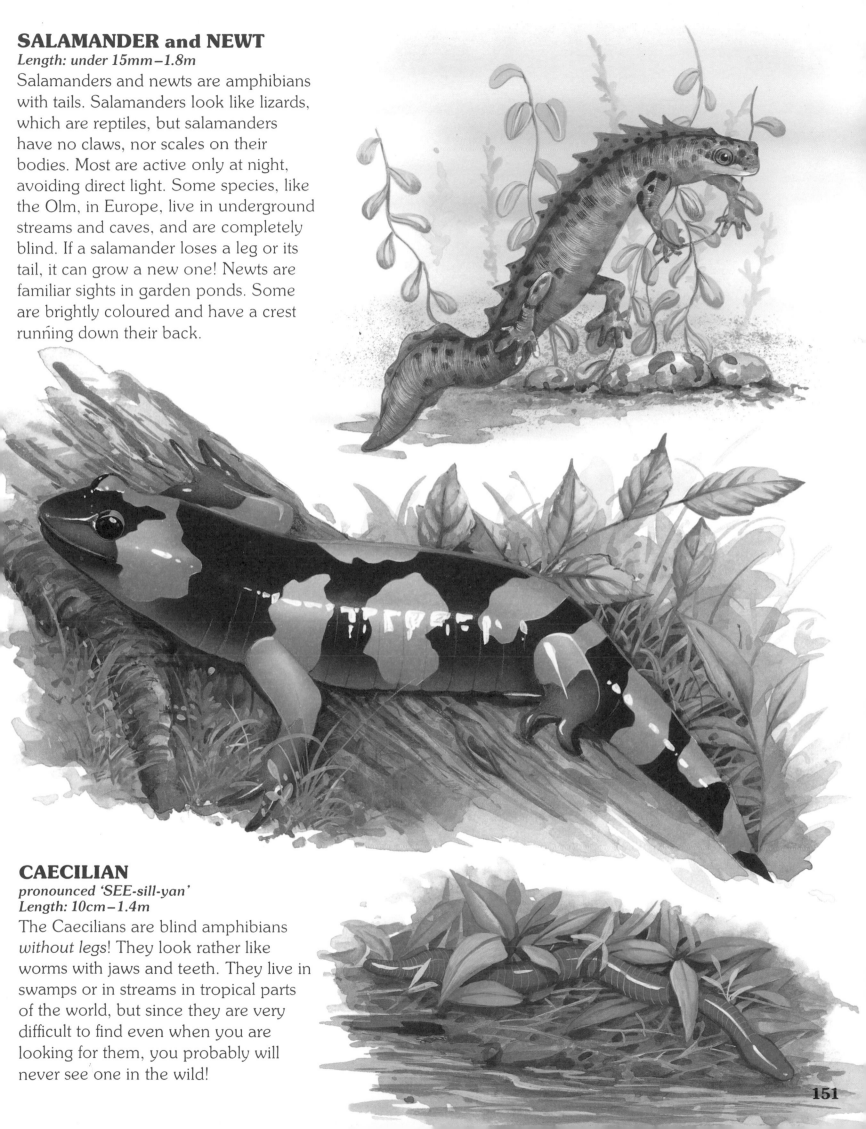

ONCE THEY RULED THE WORLD: REPTILES

Reptiles evolved from amphibians. For a long period of 160 million years in earth's history, reptiles were the dominant form of life on the planet, and existed in an enormous variety of shapes and sizes. We still do not really understand why their reign ended about 65 million years ago. Shown here are some of the reptiles in our world today.

CROCODILE and ALLIGATOR
Length: from 1m–7m

The crocodile family includes alligators, caymans, and gavials, and is descended almost unchanged in 65 million years from its dinosaur ancestors. To tell a crocodile from an alligator, look at them when the jaws are closed. If the fourth tooth from the front is sticking out, it's a crocodile! All have rough skins, long, strong tails, and are superb swimmers. The Nile Crocodile lives in the great River Nile in Africa. It often sleeps in the sun with its mouth open, while birds called plovers hop in and out, cleaning its teeth! Herodotus, a Greek historian and voyager, first mentioned this in his writings 2,500 years ago!

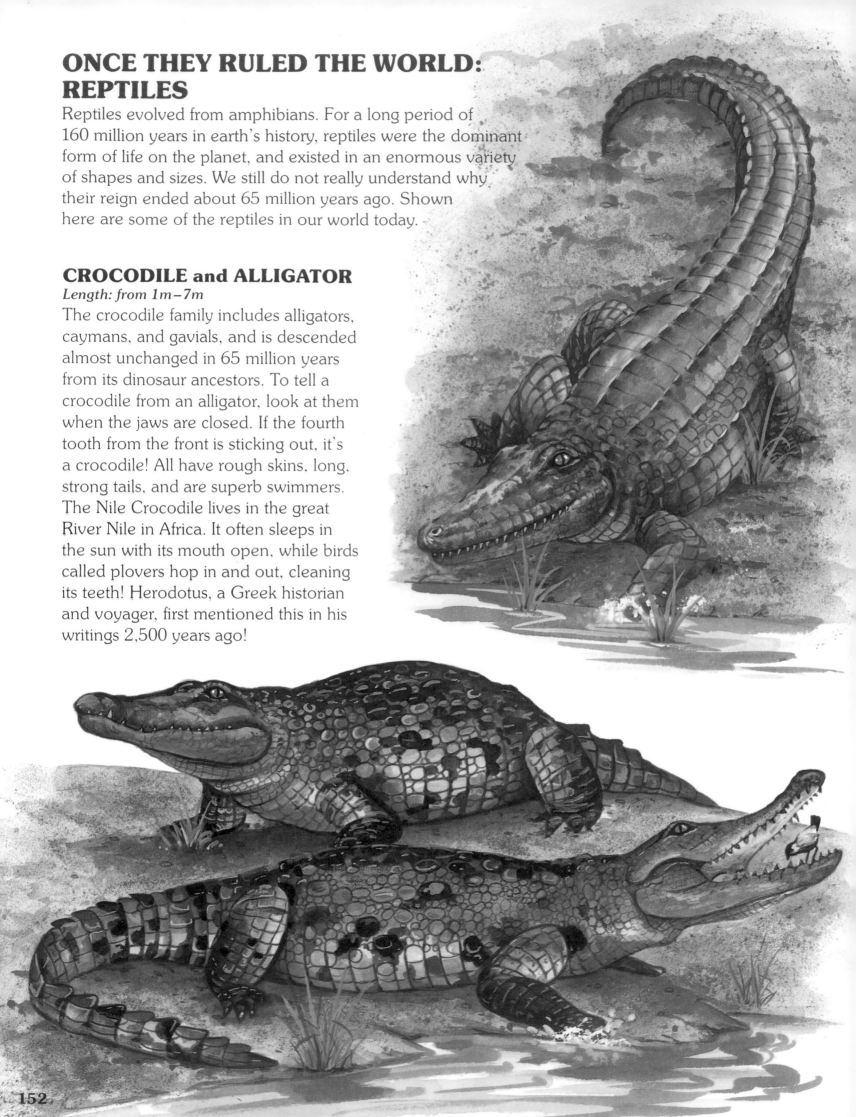

LIZARD

Length: 18mm–3.1m

Except in very cold areas, lizards live all over the world, ranging in size from tiny Geckos in Central America to the dragon-like Komodo Monitors in Indonesia. The Australian Thorny Devil is protected by the sharp spines on its back, and the South American Basilisk Lizard can actually run across water for several metres on its back legs! The Draco of South-East Asia 'flies', or glides, from tree to tree, thanks to flaps along its sides. All lizards have cold blood, and dry, scaly, watertight skin.

SNAKE

Length: 10cm–10m

There are about 2,500 different species of snake, and 300 have poisonous bites, though only about 50 are dangerous to man, causing around 40,000 deaths each year. Sea snakes are much more venomous than those on land. Snakes have no ears, but 'hear' through sensing vibrations on the ground. Their jaws are not hinged like ours, but can open wide enough to swallow something that is many times larger than their own head! The heaviest snake of all is the Anaconda, which can weigh over 225kg.

WINGS, FEATHERS AND BEAKS: BIRDS

Only birds have feathers, and all adult birds have feathers, even if they cannot fly! Feathers are light, and the bones of most birds are hollow, which keeps their weight down, making it easier for them to get off the ground. Out of around 8,600 species of birds, most are small. They are present all over the world, except at the poles or in the deep sea. Birds lay eggs, and have warm blood. Without the sounds of birds, our world would be a much poorer place.

NIGHTINGALE
Length: about 16.5cm

The Thrush family contains some of the world's most beloved songbirds, like the blackbird, the robin, the songthrush…and the nightingale. Nightingales pass the winter in Africa, returning to Europe for the spring and summer. Only the male bird sings, but, in the spring, when singing to attract a female, the nightingale's song is unforgettable, and much loved by poets!

SWAN
Length: up to 1.5m

The long-necked swans are waterfowl, the largest and most gracious, but in the same family as geese and ducks.
There are 10 species. Best-known is the Mute Swan, so often seen on our rivers and ponds. It is not really mute, since it can make hissing noises, but it is very bad-tempered, so you are advised not to go too close! Mute Swans were domesticated in England more than 800 years ago.

BIRDS OF PARADISE
Length: up to 46cm

When the only ship to survive the first round-the-world voyage returned to Spain in 1522, it brought back two bird of paradise skins. The Spaniards were sure that such a beautiful bird could only live in paradise! Today, there are 43 species, all living in South-East Asia. It is only the male bird that has the gorgeous display of plumage, to attract females.

EAGLE
Length: up to 1m

Eagles, with their hooked beaks, are great birds of prey. The Golden Eagle was a symbol of the power of Ancient Rome, and an image of the bird was carried on a staff before each legion in the Roman army. The Bald Eagle, the national bird of the United States, eats fish. If it cannot catch its own, it steals from other birds! It is not really bald. Its head and neck are covered in white feathers. Its nests are the biggest of all bird's-nests, measuring as much as 6 metres wide by nearly 3 metres deep!

OUR KIND OF ANIMAL: MAMMALS

Mammals are warm-blooded animals, with bodies completely, or partly, covered in hair. Their newborn young are fed on their mothers' milk. Mammals are widespread on land. Bats are flying mammals. Whales, dolphins, and porpoises are marine mammals. Man is a mammal, and his closest relatives are monkeys, which have tails, and apes, like gorillas and chimpanzees, which are tail-less.

CHIMPANZEE

Height: up to 1.3m

Of all the apes, the chimpanzee most resembles us. Their body is covered in hair, though the face is not. Chimpanzees live in the forests of central Africa, travelling in groups of up to 20 individuals, with a male leader. They are unusual animals, since they can use tools, employing twigs for fishing and stones as hammers. Sadly, because they are so intelligent and like us, we use many chimpanzees for experiments in our laboratories.

LION

Weight: up to 313kg

Lions are members of the cat family, the only cats to live and hunt in groups, called 'prides'. A pride of lions consists of related females and young, with one or two adult males. Generally, it is the lionesses who do the hunting, but after the prey is killed, the lions eat first, followed by the lionesses, with the cubs feeding last of all! They are carnivores, or flesh-eaters. Nowadays, they survive in the wild only in East Africa, and in one small part of India.

SEAL
Weight: up to 4,000kg

The 19 species of seals are carnivorous mammals that live in water. All are furry, with a thick layer of fat, called blubber, beneath the skin. The Grey Seal is a common sight off the coasts of Europe and North America. Weddell Seals live in the bitter Antarctic Ocean, where the sea freezes over. In order to breathe, they have to chew holes in the ice! The largest seal is the Elephant Seal, growing to over 6.5 metres in length. It gets its name from the 30cm-long 'trunk' on the male's head, which it inflates when it is excited.

DUCK-BILLED PLATYPUS
Length: up to 75cm

This is one of the most primitive mammals. Its fur-covered head, body and tail are flattened. Its eyes, like a reptile, are on the sides of its head, it has webbed feet, and a duck-like beak. And it lays eggs! After its young hatch out, they lick milk from the fur on their mother's stomach. The platypus lives in the rivers of Australia and Tasmania. It sleeps by day in burrows which can be over 30 metres deep, and hunts worms and shrimps by night.

157

FAVOURITE PETS

The first animals to be tamed by man were almost certainly dogs…perhaps as long as 50,000 years ago! Men have kept sheep and goats for at least the last 12,000 years. 5,000 years ago, horses were tamed, and 4,000 years ago, cats were kept as pets in Ancient Egypt. Today, all over the world, all kinds of people keep animals, not just for the work they can do for us, but because we like having them around as pets. Cats and dogs are among the favourites.

CAT
Weight: from 1.8 – 9.07kg

The cat purring on your lap belongs to the same family as the lion and the tiger. More than 4,000 years ago, in Ancient Egypt, cats were gods. People were forbidden to harm them. When a cat died, it was wrapped in spices and special cloth, turned into a mummy, and given a public funeral. Only 100 years ago, in one place in Egypt, someone discovered 300,000 ancient, cat mummies! Our tabbies today are direct descendants of those sacred cats. Persian Cats have long hair, Siamese have short hair (and loud voices), and Manx Cats have no tails. All have excellent eyesight, especially in dim light, and long, sharp claws on the ends of their toes, which can be pulled back into sheaths when not in use.

DOG
Height to shoulder: from 6.3cm–1.05m

Wolves, jackals, and foxes are wild dogs. The pet dogs in our homes today are all originally descended from wild dogs which were first tamed by men, long, long ago. There are over 400 different types of dog, ranging from tiny Yorkshire Terriers to enormous Great Danes. Many people prefer a certain type, or breed, of dog, perhaps a poodle, or a spaniel, or a bulldog. But most of us end up by losing our hearts to a friendly 'mutt' of no particular breed at all…in other words, a mongrel!

WORKING ANIMALS

Some animals have to work hard for us, pulling or carrying heavy loads, or people. They are known as the 'beasts of burden'. Shown here are a few of these patient animals from different parts of the world.

HORSE
Height: up to 1.98m

Apart from the horses that carry men on their backs, for the last 500 years or more big carthorses have pulled ploughs, and carted heavy loads for us. The word 'horsepower' is even used as a measurement of an engine's strength. Originally, these powerful horses were bred to carry the weight of a knight in full armour. Nowadays, the Shire is the tallest, and the most gentle, of workhorses. The Percheron and the Clydesdale are other popular breeds. Tractors do most of their farm work now, but carthorses are still with us.

CAMEL
Height: 2.25m

The camel is called 'the ship of the desert', because of its ability to carry both men and heavy loads across sandy wastes. A strong camel can cover nearly 50 kilometres a day with up to 450 kilograms on its back. There are two species, both well adapted for desert life, with broad, flat feet that do not sink into the sand. The Bactrian, or Asian, Camel has two humps on its back for storing fat, the Arabian Camel, or dromedary, only one. Camels eat any vegetation, and can go without drinking for days. They have strong teeth, and when angry, they spit!

DONKEY
Average height: 1.35m

The patient, long-eared donkey, plodding along under a heavy load, is descended from the African ass, a rare type of wild horse. Donkeys have been beasts of burden for man for longer than any other animal. Neither as swift nor as strong as horses, donkeys have great endurance, are more surefooted in mountains, and live twice as long! They are also cheaper to feed, eating dry vegetation. So the donkey can be always found working hard in poorer parts of the world, where people cannot afford a horse.

HIGH-SPEED ANIMALS

The fastest human athletes can reach speeds of just over 43 kilometres per hour. The fastest land animal can more than double that! The fastest bird can fly more than seven times faster! Shown here are four high-speed animals.

PEREGRINE FALCON

Length: about 45cm

This bird of prey can be found all over the world, though its numbers are declining because the widespread use of pesticides is affecting the hatching of its eggs. Peregrine falcons hunt from high in the air, swooping down on other birds at tremendous speeds. A diving peregrine is the fastest living creature, and can reach speeds of 350 kilometres an hour. The falcon strikes its prey cleanly with its talons, killing it instantly.

CHEETAH

Weight: up to 65kg

Though it is actually a big cat, the cheetah, or hunting leopard, has much in common with dogs! It does not climb, it has long legs, and it hunts by running down its prey, rather than stalking and pouncing on it, as other cats do. When chasing antelopes, the cheetah can achieve speeds of over 100 kilometres an hour, but only for a few hundred metres. It survives now only in some parts of Africa.

HUMMINGBIRD
Length: 6.0–21.6mm

The hummingbirds of North and South America are the most colourful of all birds, tiny jewels who depend for their food entirely on flowers. They are also the supreme fliers of the bird world, able just as easily to dart about, stop suddenly, hang in the air, and even fly backwards! Though they are not the world's speediest fliers, their wings beat so quickly, up to 90 times a second, that they are just a blur to our eyes. It is the humming noise of their wings which gives these birds their name.

PRONGHORN ANTELOPE
Weight: up to 65kg

Over longer distances than the cheetah, the pronghorn antelope can run at over 88 kilometres per hour. Once these small animals lived in great herds all over western North America, but most were killed in the last century by white hunters. The pronghorn antelope gets its name from the fact that it is the only member of the antelope family with divided, or pronged, horns.

163

ANIMALS IN ARMOUR

Animals have different ways of keeping out of trouble. Some can run very fast away from it. Some are so well camouflaged that they are difficult to find. Some take refuge up in trees, or vanish into holes in the ground. And there are a few animals who don't have to worry much about any trouble! They live inside their own armour-plating!

TORTOISE and TURTLE
Weight: Tortoise up to 298kg: Turtle 960kg

Tortoises and turtles belong to the same family. Species living on land are called tortoises: those living in fresh or seawater are called turtles. They are the oldest type of living reptiles, having been on earth for over 170 million years, with very little change in some cases! Most have hard shells, into which they can pull their head, legs, and tail, for protection. All lay their eggs in sand, leaving them to be hatched out by the sun's heat. Their toothless jaws form a hard beak, and they live to a great age, over 150 years in one instance!

ARMADILLO
Weight: 90g–55kg

Any animal that hopes to make a meal of an armadillo has problems, for the armadillo's back, head, sides, and tail are covered in bony armour! In addition, when attacked, some armadillos roll into a tight ball, while others dig quickly out of sight in the ground. Most armadillos live in South America, a few as far north as the southern United States. They live in groups in burrows, and are mainly insect-eaters, with lots of tiny teeth. Giant Armadillos have almost 100 teeth, more than any other mammal.

RHINOCEROS
Weight: up to 3,900kg

The only land animal larger than the rhinoceros is the elephant. A rhino can be over 2m high, and nearly 5m long! Its thick, folded skin is as tough as armour-plating, and depending on its species, it will have one or two horns on its nose. When angered, rhinos can charge at up to 40km/h, and there is a record of one derailing a train! Yet this strange-looking, short-sighted animal is actually a shy vegetarian! Most rhinos lead solitary lives; they bathe a lot, and can swim well.

FINDING FOOD IN THE DARK

Many animals are active at night, sometimes hunting their prey in almost total darkness. With some of them, their eyes are enormous, out of all proportion to the size of their bodies, to help them make the best possible use of whatever dim light that there might be. Others, though, can find food very successfully without using their eyes at all!

BAT

Wingspan: 1.6–183cm

There are about 950 species of bats. They are the only flying mammals, with wings of skin stretched between the bones of their hands and their hind legs. Most eat insects and fruit, some eat meat or fish. Vampire bats drink the blood from shallow cuts made by their sharp teeth, on cattle, poultry or even men! We say someone is as 'blind as a bat', but no bats are blind. Many bats use echo-location to 'see' in the dark. They make sounds that we cannot hear, and the echo tells them where there are obstacles…or where their prey is.

TARSIER

Weight: about 170g

Tarsiers live in the forests of South-east Asia. They have enormous, owl-like eyes, short front legs, and long back legs. They jump like frogs. Tarsiers are only 15cm long, plus a 25cm-long tail, yet even on the ground they can jump distances of nearly 2m! They are good climbers, having adhesive pads on the tips of their long fingers. They hunt at night for insects, lizards, and fish. Scientists believe it is from creatures like the tarsier that, many millions of years ago, the process of development first began that has led to man.

OWL
Height: 13–71cm

Land-dwelling birds of prey living all
over the world, with their flat faces,
hooked beaks, big eyes, and soft
feathers, owls are unmistakable. They
have remarkable hearing, and their eyes
are enormous. The Snowy Owl is only
about 60cm high, yet its eyeball is as
big as a man's! No wonder they can *see*
so well in the dark! Because of their
loose feathers, their necks seem short.
In fact, they are long and very flexible,
and the head can turn three-quarters
way round a circle! Owls hunt insects,
small mammals, birds, and fish.

GULPER EEL
Length: up to 61cm

Gulper Eels are not related to eels at all!
This strange fish lives in the darkness of
the sea's depths. Its mouth is so vast
that it is bigger than the rest of its body,
which is small! Its tiny eyes are at the
tip of its snout, and it has a long tail, with a luminous tip, to attract other
fish. The teeth of the Gulper Eel point backwards, so nothing can escape after
entering its mouth!

MASTERS OF DISGUISE

The skins or coats of many animals are coloured in ways that make them difficult to see. This 'disguise' helps them to blend into the background, so that they can hide from hunters. And, if they are hunters themselves, a good disguise gives them more chance of catching their next meal! Some animals change their skin colour according to what they happen to be standing on at the time! Some, for survival, 'copy' the appearance of another creature.

TIGER

Weight: up to 423kg

Tigers are the largest members of the cat family. Once, they ranged widely over Asia, but now there are probably only about 3,000 tigers living in the wild. They are spectacular to look at, and graceful in their movements. They keep to the dark forests, sleeping by day, and hunting deer and pigs by night. With their striped coats, they are almost impossible to see against a jungle background when they are standing still. Unlike most cats, tigers love bathing.

ZEBRA

Height: up to 1.6m

Zebras are stocky wild horses, with distinctive, black and white striped markings. There are 3 species, feeding on grass on the open plains or in lightly wooded areas in the east and south of the African continent. The zebra's stripes break up its outline very effectively, making it hard to spot against a background of sun-dappled, tall grass.

CHAMELEON

Length: 3.8–63.5cm

Chameleons are found in Africa, Arabia, and India. They can change colour in an instant, to blend in with their background, or when they are frightened. Each of their eyes can move independently, and they are capable of looking in any direction. Chameleons feed on insects, catching them on a sticky tongue, which they can shoot out further than the length of their own head and body combined!

MONARCH BUTTERFLY

Wingspan: up to 10cm

and VICEROY BUTTERFLY

Wingspan: up to 7.5cm

The Viceroy Butterfly is a perfect example of another form of disguise, called mimicry, where one animal mimics, or copies, the appearance of another. Birds eat butterflies, but avoid the Monarch because its blood tastes foul to them. The wing pattern of the Viceroy closely resembles the Monarch's wing pattern. So, although it would taste good to them, because it looks like a Monarch, birds leave the Viceroy Butterfly alone as well!

169

THE LARGEST ON LAND

Although the biggest of all the animals live in the sea (see page 172),
there are some very large creatures on the land. Each of those shown
below is unusual, not just in its size, but in some other way as well.
The giraffe and the hippopotamus are found only in Africa. The
elephant can be found in both Africa and Asia.

ELEPHANT
Height at shoulder:
up to 4.2m

The two species, the African Elephant and the Indian Elephant, are highly
intelligent vegetarians, the largest living land animals. The African Elephant is
the larger, weighing up to 12 tonnes, and has bigger ears. An elephant's nose
is extended to form a trunk, used for breathing, grasping things, drinking,
and fighting. On each side of that are their tusks, enormous teeth, sometimes
3m long. Other teeth are also huge, some 10cm wide by 25cm long! For
giant animals, elephants walk very softly, because their feet are padded.

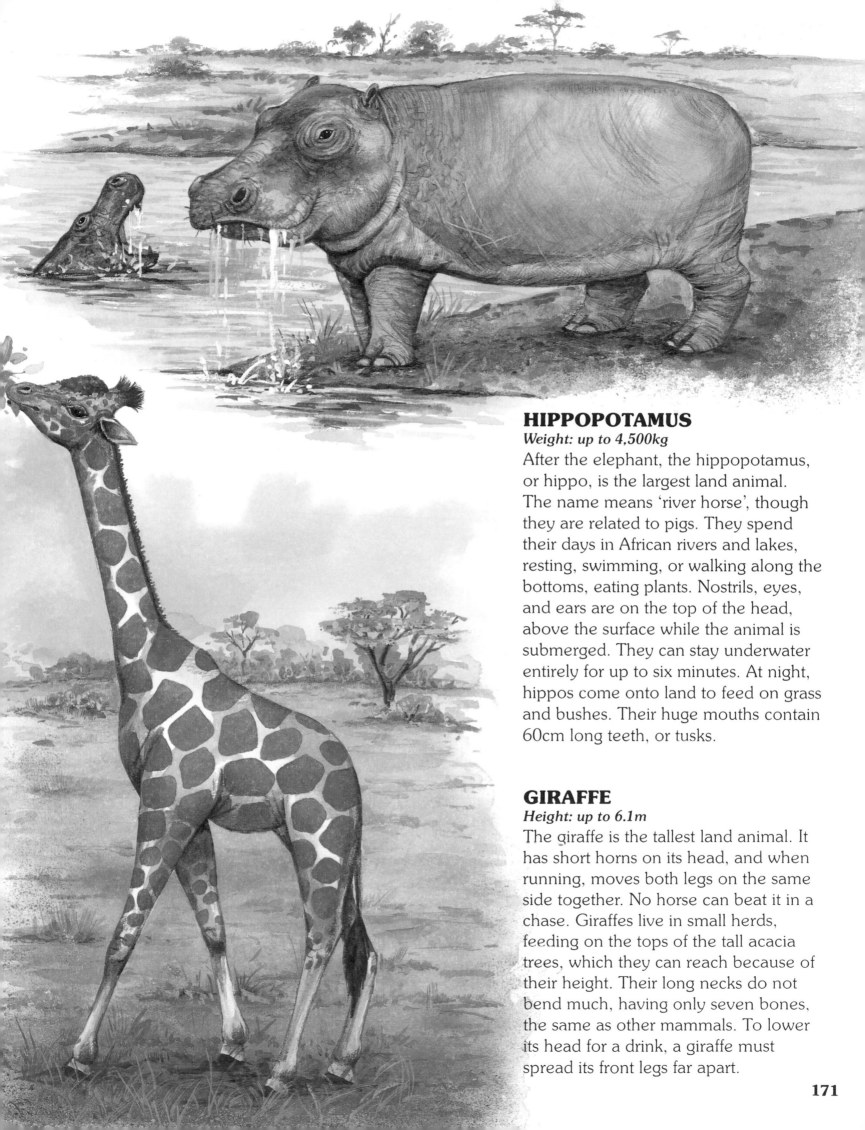

HIPPOPOTAMUS
Weight: up to 4,500kg

After the elephant, the hippopotamus, or hippo, is the largest land animal. The name means 'river horse', though they are related to pigs. They spend their days in African rivers and lakes, resting, swimming, or walking along the bottoms, eating plants. Nostrils, eyes, and ears are on the top of the head, above the surface while the animal is submerged. They can stay underwater entirely for up to six minutes. At night, hippos come onto land to feed on grass and bushes. Their huge mouths contain 60cm long teeth, or tusks.

GIRAFFE
Height: up to 6.1m

The giraffe is the tallest land animal. It has short horns on its head, and when running, moves both legs on the same side together. No horse can beat it in a chase. Giraffes live in small herds, feeding on the tops of the tall acacia trees, which they can reach because of their height. Their long necks do not bend much, having only seven bones, the same as other mammals. To lower its head for a drink, a giraffe must spread its front legs far apart.

171

GIANTS IN THE SEA

Some animals that live on the land can grow to a great size, but they are dwarfed by the creatures that live in the sea. Here are four marine giants. The largest of all, the Blue Whale, is a mammal.

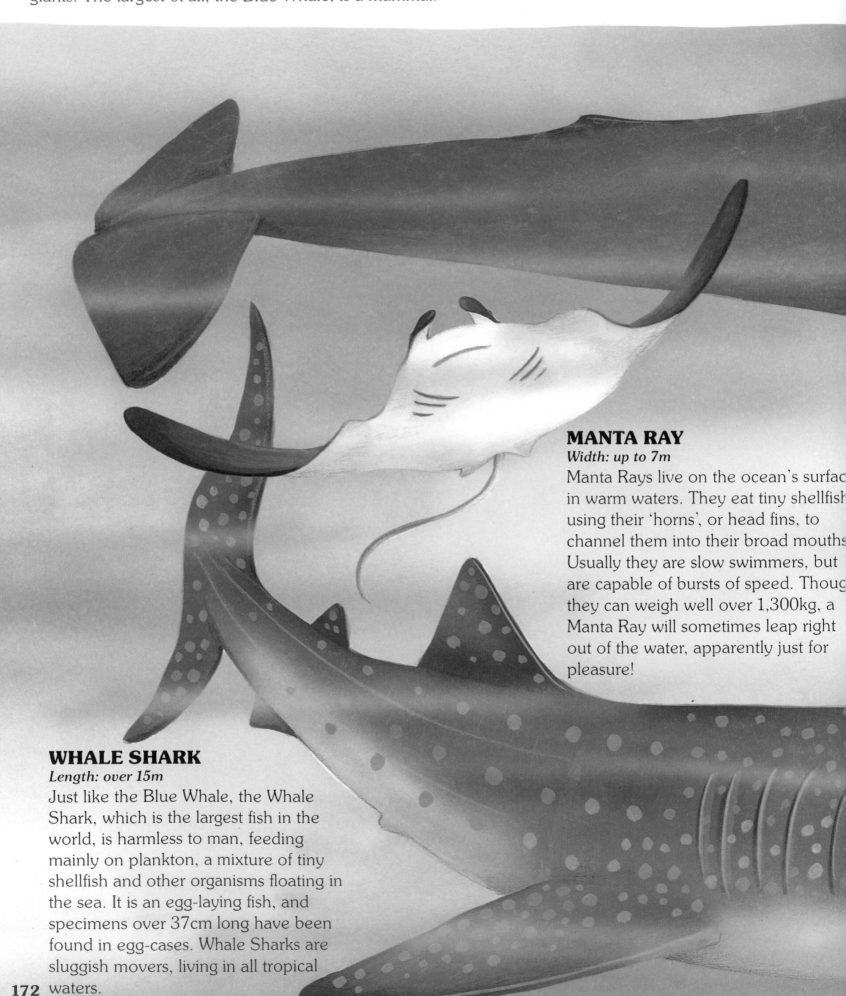

MANTA RAY
Width: up to 7m

Manta Rays live on the ocean's surface in warm waters. They eat tiny shellfish using their 'horns', or head fins, to channel them into their broad mouths. Usually they are slow swimmers, but are capable of bursts of speed. Though they can weigh well over 1,300kg, a Manta Ray will sometimes leap right out of the water, apparently just for pleasure!

WHALE SHARK
Length: over 15m

Just like the Blue Whale, the Whale Shark, which is the largest fish in the world, is harmless to man, feeding mainly on plankton, a mixture of tiny shellfish and other organisms floating in the sea. It is an egg-laying fish, and specimens over 37cm long have been found in egg-cases. Whale Sharks are sluggish movers, living in all tropical waters.

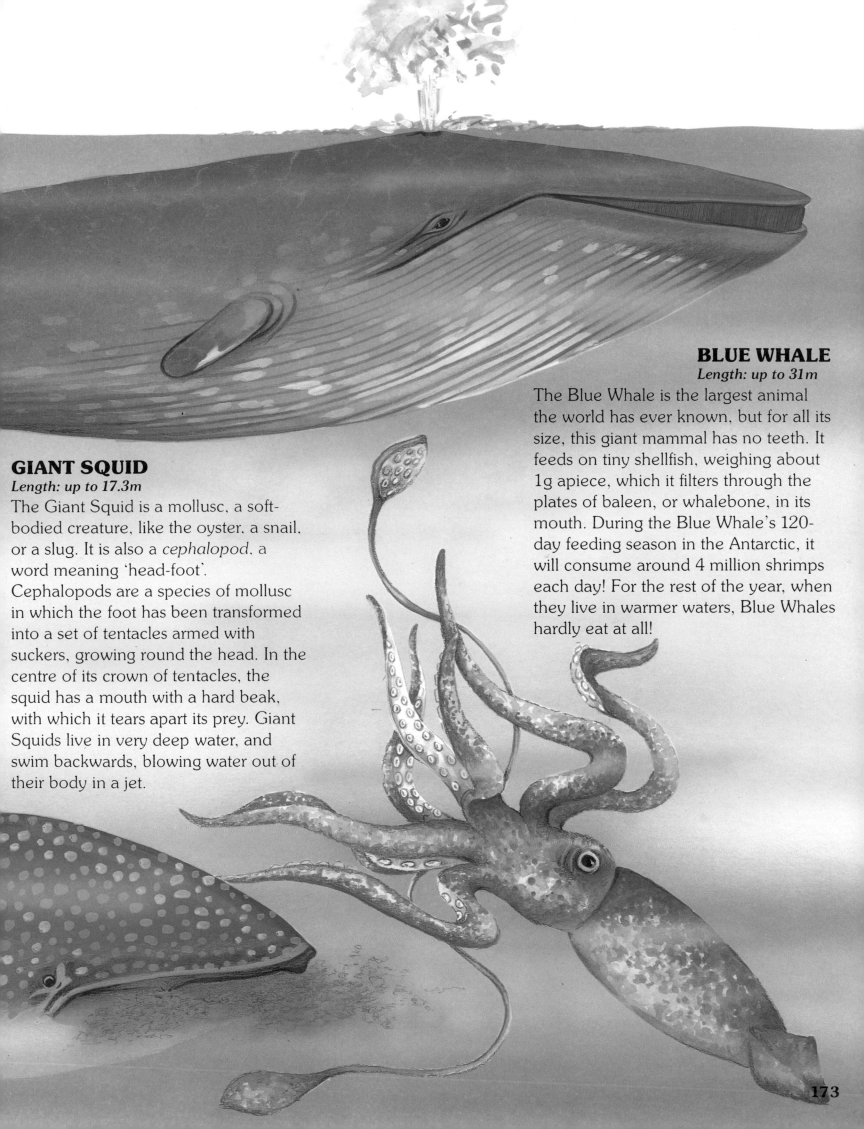

BLUE WHALE
Length: up to 31m

The Blue Whale is the largest animal the world has ever known, but for all its size, this giant mammal has no teeth. It feeds on tiny shellfish, weighing about 1g apiece, which it filters through the plates of baleen, or whalebone, in its mouth. During the Blue Whale's 120-day feeding season in the Antarctic, it will consume around 4 million shrimps each day! For the rest of the year, when they live in warmer waters, Blue Whales hardly eat at all!

GIANT SQUID
Length: up to 17.3m

The Giant Squid is a mollusc, a soft-bodied creature, like the oyster, a snail, or a slug. It is also a *cephalopod*, a word meaning 'head-foot'. Cephalopods are a species of mollusc in which the foot has been transformed into a set of tentacles armed with suckers, growing round the head. In the centre of its crown of tentacles, the squid has a mouth with a hard beak, with which it tears apart its prey. Giant Squids live in very deep water, and swim backwards, blowing water out of their body in a jet.

REMARKABLE INSECTS

Insects are very adaptable. Few of them live in the sea, but apart from that, they have conquered almost everywhere else. One kind of an insect or another will eat almost anything; from dung to solid wood to blood. Some of the more remarkable members of the Insect family are shown here.

STICK-INSECT

Length: up to 33cm

The Giant Stick-Insect of Indonesia is the longest insect in the world. Stick-Insects look so much like twigs on the trees they live on that they are almost impossible to detect. They move and feed only by night, remaining motionless during the day. Few stick-insects are male, since the females lay fertile eggs without mating.

PRAYING MANTIS

Length: about 5cm

The name of this insect comes from its habit of holding its spiny forelegs folded like hands in prayer. A Praying Mantis will sit motionless in this position for long periods…until some unsuspecting victim comes close enough to be caught and devoured. They will even eat each other if they get the chance!

FIREFLY
Body Length: about 1cm

Fireflies are actually softwinged beetles, with light-producing organs on the body. At night, male fireflies fly about giving out a brilliant light, while the females sit in the grass responding with a fainter light. The light is cold, since the firefly can convert energy to light much more efficiently than our own electric light bulbs, for instance, which waste in the form of heat most of the energy needed to make them work.

BOMBARDIER BEETLE
Length: about 1cm

This beetle is a long-legged, fast-running hunter, one of a group known as ground beetles. The Bombardier Beetle gets its name from its defensive behaviour. When alarmed, it will fire out of its rear end, with a small bang, hot, corrosive liquid at an attacker!

CICADA
Body Length: about 3.5cm

A Cicada is a plant-feeding bug, with a long, piercing beak which is folded back under the head when not in use. The male Cicada is the loudest of all the insects, capable of producing a sound, by vibrating tiny membranes in the side of its body, which can be heard over 400m away.

SLEEPING THROUGH THE WINTER

Some animals sleep all through the winter months. This sleep is called 'hibernation'. Reptiles hibernate in cold weather because they would freeze to death if they stayed out in the open. Some warm-blooded mammals sleep through the winter because it is hard for them to find food when there is snow and ice on the ground. Animals that hibernate eat a lot before they hibernate, so that their body fat will keep them alive while they are having their long sleep.

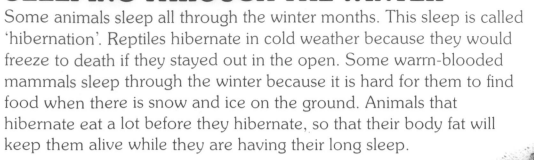

FAT DORMOUSE
Body Length: about 16cm

The Fat Dormouse lives over most of Europe, and is the largest European dormouse. It looks rather like a small grey squirrel. They come out of their nests, usually at night, to feed on fruit, nuts, and insects. Before their winter sleep, they are very fat, and the Ancient Romans ate them, which is why they are also called the Edible Dormouse!

KODIAK BEAR
Weight: up to 730kg

This bear gets its name from Kodiak Island near the south-western coast of Alaska, where it is found. The Kodiak Bear is the world's largest living carnivore, or flesh-eater. It belongs to a group of bears known as brown bears, like the Grizzly Bear. These bears sleep through most of the winter in individual dens, but may wake up if the weather becomes warm.

HEDGEHOG
Length: about 25cm

Hedgehogs live in woodland, and also in our gardens. Our best chances of seeing them are during twilight or at night. They will patter around then in search of food, and though they are mainly insect-eaters, they will actually take almost anything edible. When threatened, they roll into a prickly ball. Hedgehogs hibernate in winter.

MARMOT

Weight: about 8kg

Marmots are stout-bodied animals, with rounded ears and strong digging claws. They are plant-eating rodents, related to squirrels and chipmunks. Marmots live in colonies in burrows on south-facing mountain slopes, above the tree-line. 'Sentries' keep guard during the day, sitting up on their haunches, and give a shrill whistle at a sign of danger, sending the whole colony underground in an instant. The colony hibernates in winter.

FLIGHTLESS BIRDS

Most birds have breastbones that are shaped like the keel of a boat, and the birds' flying muscles are attached to this. Some birds, though, over a period of millions of years, have stopped using their wings, and their breastbones have flattened out and now look like rafts rather than keels. The Latin word for raft is *ratis*, so these birds are called ratite birds. Birds like penguins, though they do not fly, use their 'flying' muscles for swimming, so their breastbones are still shaped like keels, and they are not ratites. Ratites are the largest birds in the world.

OSTRICH

Height: up to 2.74m

The largest birds in the world live in the sandy wastes and on the thornbush-covered plains of Africa. There, they overlook every animal except the giraffe. They are also swift runners, capable of speeds of up to 64km/h. If cornered, an Ostrich will kick out with its powerful legs. Their claws are strong enough to damage a lion or a man. A fully-grown male Ostrich can weigh over 155kg, and an egg was once laid that weighed 2.3kg, big enough to provide about 20 people with a scrambled egg breakfast!

EMU

Height: about 1.8m

The Emu lives in Australia, and, after the ostrich, is the second-largest bird in the world. It is a nomadic, or wandering, species, and some individual Emus have been known to travel 1,000km in a year. These birds can cause considerable damage to crops, and in 1932 the state of Western Australia recruited the help of an army machine-gun unit to destroy them. But the birds scattered each time the soldiers opened fire, and the 'Emu War' was abandoned after a month.

CASSOWARY

Height: up to 1.6m

There are two species of Cassowary, both living in New Guinea, a large island to the north of Australia. They do not fly, and have blue and red skin on their heads and necks. Cassowaries also have a bony helmet, or casque, on the top of their head, which protects them as they race head-first through the undergrowth. The Dwarf Cassowary is regarded as the most dangerous bird in the world. Before nesting, the female will attack any creature nearby with its viciously-sharp, 10cm long claw.

KIWI

Height: up to 70cm

The thin, piping *kee-wee* cry of this bird echoing through the swampy forests of New Zealand is said to be the origin of its name. The largest Kiwi is about the size of a fat hen, and they are very difficult to see in the wild, being small, brown, and active only at night. Most birds have nostrils at the base of their bills, but, with Kiwis, the nostrils are at the very tip.

179

STRANGE SEA CREATURES

Much more of the earth's surface is covered by the sea than by the land. The sea also is richer in different forms of animal life than either dry land or freshwater. Shown below are four of these varied forms of life, each of them 'strange' in some way.

OCTOPUS

Arm span: up to 9.5m

Like the squid (see page 32), the octopus is a *cephalopod*, a mollusc with eight tentacles around its mouth. On each tentacle are two rows of suction cups, with which it picks up the crabs and shellfish on which it lives, bringing them to its mouth to be crushed by its strong beak. The female Octopus lays her eggs in her cave home, then remains with them, guarding them and circulating water over them, until the young are hatched.

STARFISH

Spread: up to 1m

The Starfish is not a fish at all! It is an *echinoderm*, which means a 'spiny-skinned' animal, just like Sea Urchins and Sea Cucumbers. The Common Starfish has five arms, but some kinds have up to 50, but always the number is a multiple of 5! The mouth is underneath the body, surrounded by tube feet which are covered in little suckers. When the Starfish attacks an oyster, it fastens its feet to each side of the shell, and then, slowly, pulls it apart. Eventually, it is opened enough for the Starfish to turn its own stomach inside out, and slide it into the shell, to eat the oyster within!

PORTUGESE MAN-OF-WAR

Length: up to 12.2m

The Portugese Man-of-War is a jellyfish, that is actually composed of a whole colony of tiny animals! Some of them eat and digest food; some act as fishing lines, catching fish; others are useful only for feeling. The float or 'sail' is a gas-filled bag that drives the colony across the ocean. When a fish touches the long, trailing tentacles underneath, poison shoots out of tiny darts. Then the fish is grabbed by the tentacles, lifted up, and eaten. This jellyfish got its name because it reminded sailors of a battleship sailing along, with darts for guns.

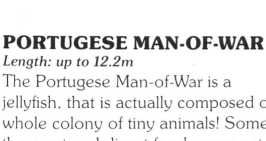

STONEFISH

Length: up to 60cm

This ugly fish can be found in shallow, inshore waters in the Indian and Pacific Oceans, especially around coral reefs. Its rough skin and drab colouring make it very difficult to see when it is resting on the bottom, which is unfortunate, because it is the most poisonous fish in the world! Direct contact with its spines can kill a man, slowly and painfully.

LIVING IN THE TREES

Trees are essential to life on earth because of the part they play in renewing the air that we breathe. In addition, an extraordinarily wide variety of animals actually dwell in the trees. Shown here are four different animals that find food, shelter, and everything that they need up in the treetops.

SLOTH

Length: up to 60cm

The Sloth will sleep hanging upside down from a tree-branch for as many as 19 hours a day. And it moves only slowly even when 'active', perhaps covering around 3 metres in a minute in a tree, and rather less when on the ground. The Sloth's hair grows in the opposite direction to the hair on other mammals, from the abdomen to the back, so that rain is shed effectively even when the creature is upside down. Sloths live solitary lives in the tropical forests of Central and South America. Their bodies are remarkably strong, and even serious wounds will heal quickly.

HOWLER MONKEY

Weight: up to 9kg

Howler Monkeys are found throughout Central, and most of South America. They are the noisiest animals in the Amazon forest, and their cries can be heard over distances of 3km! They have a thick, coarse coat, but a bald face, and a bulging throat from which comes the loud roar. Up to 40 monkeys live together in a troop. defending their territory against other troops.

KOALA
Length: up to 80cm

The Koala is a *marsupial*, or 'pouched mammal'. A marsupial gives birth to tiny, helpless young which are then fed and sheltered in a pouch on the mother's abdomen until they are big enough to leave. Koalas are found in Australia, sleeping by day, and by night feeding exclusively on the leaves and shoots of the eucalyptus trees on which they live. The capture and export of this living 'Teddy bear' is forbidden by Australian law.

TREE FROG
Length: up to 6cm

There are over 800 species of Tree Frogs. Their toes have expanded discs at the tips which assist gripping so much that a Tree Frog can climb a vertical sheet of glass. They are strong jumpers, able to launch themselves so accurately at an insect that they can swallow it as they land. Some Tree Frogs are brightly coloured as a warning to attackers that they are very poisonous to eat.

183

THE GREAT TRAVELLERS

As the weather changes and life around them becomes more harsh, many animals, especially birds, make long and difficult journeys to other parts of the world, where they can find richer food supplies, easier living conditions, or a safer place to give birth to their young. These long journeys are called 'migrations'. Most migrations are seasonal, but there are also instances where members of a species, like the Pacific Salmon mentioned opposite, make a journey that lasts a whole lifetime.

GREY WHALE
Length: up to 15.3m

Each year, Grey Whales undertake a 20,000km journey from their feeding grounds around the Bering Straits, where the continents of Asia and North America come close to each other, to the Pacific coasts of northern Mexico, where they breed. This is the longest migration of any mammal. After four summer months in the northern seas, at the end of September each year, the move begins to Mexico, where they arrive at Christmas time. On the trip, Grey Whales travel at speeds of up to 185km a day! After the young are born, the whales set off again in February, but the return journey is slower, because of the presence of the new calves, and the effect of the currents.

PACIFIC SALMON
Weight: up to 45kg

There are 5 species of Pacific Salmon, found on the west coasts of North America from Alaska to southern California. They are born in the upper waters of the fast-moving rivers that flow into the Pacific. After one or two years of life, the young fish travel down these rivers to the sea, where they spend their adult life. Then they make their way back, across thousands of kilometres, from the far side of the Pacific Ocean, to the river waters of their birth. When they set out, they are in prime condition, but they cease eating when they enter the river mouths. The few that survive the exhausting journey, against fierce currents, over waterfalls and through rapids, without being eaten by predators or caught by fishermen, lay their eggs with the last of their strength, and then die!

ARCTIC TERN
Height: up to 38cm

When it comes to migration, of all the animals in the world, the Arctic Tern is the long-distance record-breaker! When it is summer in the northern half of the world, or 'hemisphere', Arctic Terns breed within the Arctic Circle. When winter approaches in the northern hemisphere, they fly south towards the Antarctic Circle, where it is then summer, in order to pass the other half of the year in the southern hemisphere. In a period of 10 months, one Arctic Tern is known to have flown a distance of over 22,500km! Consequently, as some of these birds both nest and winter in parts of the world where the sun never sets, they see more daylight than any other living animal!

ANIMALS AT RISK

Man's actions are leading to the extinction of more and more species of animal life. Sometimes, animals are hunted until there are so few left alive that it is impossible for them to continue breeding. Sometimes, the destruction of the animals' natural surroundings for one reason or another causes an irreversible decline in the animal population. We are leaving fewer and fewer places where wild animals can live in peace. Sometimes, the cause of the destruction of wild life is the pollution that man spreads wherever he goes. By accident or intention, we poison other living creatures to death. Unless we are content to look forward to a future without wild animals, we must do all that we can now to stop this destruction. Shown here are just four of the many animals that are at risk.

YANGTZE RIVER DOLPHIN
Length: up to 2.4m

This shy, slim, long-beaked dolphin lives in China's greatest river, the Yangtze. Chinese legends say that it is the reincarnation of a drowned princess! Of all the dolphins, whales and porpoises, the Yangtze River Dolphin is the most endangered. Though now protected by law, some still die each year through being caught up in fishing gear. There are probably only about 300 of these mammals left alive in the wild.

GIANT PANDA
Length: up to 1.5m

A relative of the raccoons and bears, the Giant Panda lives in the mountains of south-west China. It eats only bamboo, feeding for up to 16 hours a day. Pandas must consume enormous amounts of bamboo in order to stay alive. But the bamboo forests are being cut down to make way for farms, and smaller and smaller wooded areas are left. As Pandas will not cross open country, an isolated animal cannot find itself a mate in another part of the remaining forest. Unfortunately, Giant Pandas do not breed well in captivity.

OSPREY

Length: up to 60cm

The hawk-like Osprey lives entirely on fish which it catches in a spectacular way. The bird soars in circles above the water at heights of up to 60m. When it spots a target, it hovers momentarily, then plunges straight down, feet first, into the water, going right under the surface. After a few seconds, it re-emerges with the fish clutched in its feet, which have spines on them to help them grip their slippery prey. Because the seas have become so polluted, the fish that the Ospreys eat are full of poison, and the numbers of these birds are now greatly reduced.

GORILLA

Height: up to 1.88m

Gorillas are man's closest animal relatives. They live in the rainforests of west and central Africa, eating plants and berries. There are two species, the Lowland Gorilla and the shaggier Mountain Gorilla. Because of the poverty and civil wars in the countries in which they live, their habitat is fast being destroyed. There are probably no more than 300 Mountain Gorillas left alive.

INDEX

This omnibus edition first published in 2000 by Brown Watson
The Old Mill, 76 Fleckney Road,
Kibworth Beauchamp,
Leicestershire LE8 OHG

© 2000 Brown Watson, England
Printed in Slovakia
ISBN: 0-7097-1351-7